GREAT DISCOVERIES IN SCIENCE

Cloning

Cathleen Small

Cavendish Square
New York

Published in 2019 by Cavendish Square Publishing, LLC
243 5th Avenue, Suite 136, New York, NY 10016

First Edition

Library of Congress Cataloging-in-Publication Data

Names: Small, Cathleen, author.
Title: Cloning / Cathleen Small.
Description: First edition. | New York : Cavendish Square, 2019. | Series:
Great discoveries in science | Audience: Grades 9-12. | Includes bibliographical references and index.
Identifiers: LCCN 2018008861 (print) | LCCN 2018011728 (ebook) |
ISBN 9781502643759 (ebook) | ISBN 9781502643858 (library bound) | ISBN 9781502643971 (pbk.)
Subjects: LCSH: Cloning—Juvenile literature. |
Cloning—History—Juvenile literature. | Molecular cloning—Juvenile literature.
Classification: LCC QH442.2 (ebook) | LCC QH442.2 .S63 2019 (print) | DDC 660.6/5—dc23
LC record available at https://lccn.loc.gov/2018008861

Editorial Director: David McNamara
Editor: Jodyanne Benson
Copy Editor: Michele Suchomel-Casey
Associate Art Director: Alan Sliwinski
Designer: Christina Shults
Production Coordinator: Karol Szymczuk
Photo Research: J8 Media

The photographs in this book are used by permission and through the courtesy of:
Cover Obeastsofierce/Shutterstock.com; p. 4 Look and Learn/Bridgeman Images; p. 9 Juan Gaertner/Shutterstock.com; p. 10 The Print Collector/Getty Images; p. 13 Mirko Sobotta/Shutterstock.com; p. 16 Yuri Smityuk/TASS/Getty Images; p. 19 Michael Smith/Hulton Archive/Getty Images; p. 21 Kim Jae-Hwan/AFP/Getty Images; p. 26 Lukiyanova Natalia Frenta/Shutterstock.com; p. 29 KY Tan/Shutterstock.com; p. 33 KT Design/Shutterstock.com; p. 37 Designua/Shuterstock.com; p. 41 Rinaldofr/Shutterstock.com; p. 46 Imagno/Getty Images; p. 48 Natalie Jean/Shutterstock.com; p. 51 SPL/Science Source; p. 53 Shevs/Shutterstock.com; p. 59 Paul Clements/AP Images; p. 60 Jose Miguel Pintor Ortego /Wikimedia Commons/File:Celia la última bucardo.JPG/CC BY SA 4.0; p. 64 Jiang Baocheng/VCG/Getty Images; p. 66 Kevin Horan/Aurora Photos/Alamy Stock Photo; p. 68 Wikimedia Commons/File:DNA gel.jpg/Public Domain; p. 71 Fuse Bulb/Shutterstock.com; p. 78 Elena Pavlovich/Shutterstock.com; p. 81 Jin Liwang/Xinhua/Getty Images; p. 83 Jeffrey Markowitz/Sygma/Getty Images; p. 86 Rosenfeld Images Ltd./Science Source; p. 88 Dominic Lipinski/PA Images/Getty Images; p. 92 Amelie-Benoist/BSIP/Alamy Stock Photo; p. 94 Noah Berger/Bloomberg'/Getty Images; p. 95 Nissim Benvenisty/Wikimedia Commons/File:Human embryonic stem cells only A.png/CC BY 2,5; p. 100 Colin McPherson/Alamy Stock Photo.

Printed in the United States of America

Contents

In the world of science fiction, some have speculated that cloning could be used to bring back the dinosaurs.

Introduction

Cloning used to be the stuff of science fiction. Fascinating books, television shows, and movies imagined worlds where humans were cloned—sometimes for good, and sometimes for bad. In the popular book and subsequent film series *Jurassic Park*, for example, DNA recovered from dinosaurs is cloned and used to bring the dinosaurs back from extinction. In the books and the movies, the dinosaur cloning ends with disastrous results and becomes a cautionary tale that perhaps it's not the best idea to interfere with nature without thinking about possible consequences. Cloning is also a subject in several of the *Star Wars* movies and spin-offs, as well as in the popular 2009 film *Avatar*.

But in the past century, cloning has become a reality—not necessarily in the way it's depicted in movies, books, and television, but sometimes in similar ways. For example, reproductive cloning has been used to attempt to bring back extinct species, but not dinosaurs. (Scientists believe any dinosaur DNA they could recover would likely be too degraded to effectively create a clone. Also, reproductive cloning of animals requires a host mother to carry the animal and birth it, and it's questionable what currently living animal would be a suitable host for a dinosaur embryo.)

Some uses of cloning actually would make for great science fiction! One of the primary areas of cloning research today is in cloning stem cells. The human body is made up of cells, but in an adult, nearly all the cells are differentiated, meaning they specialize in certain functions. For example, skin cells are differentiated—that is, they function to create and maintain skin tissue. They do *not* do the job of, for example, stomach cells, which are differentiated to perform and maintain the functions of that part of the digestive tract.

Cells don't start out differentiated, though. In the very earliest stages of development, right after an egg is fertilized, the first cells that replicate in the embryo are stem cells. They are not yet differentiated, and thus, they can theoretically perform nearly any function. As the embryo develops, the cells begin to differentiate. The functions the cells do not need are turned off. For example, functions for anything other than creating and maintaining the skin are turned off in skin cells.

So, in theory, if scientists can harvest and clone stem cells, they can create stores of very versatile cells that can be used for many different functions. For example, if a person has some type of diseased tissue in his or her body, stem cells could be used to generate new, healthy tissue to repair the diseased tissue.

There are a couple of problems with this, though. First, unless the cells come from the person with the diseased tissue, the body may reject the new cells. Second, because the greatest number of stem cells—and the most versatile stem cells—come from embryos, there is an ethical debate about whether they should be used. Until recently, harvesting embryonic stem cells meant destroying the embryo, which many determined was the same as destroying a life. New developments in the field, though, have opened up possibilities for harvesting embryonic stem cells without destroying embryos.

Stem-cell cloning is at the forefront of medical research, and the possible therapeutic uses for stem cells are numerous. As research continues, scientists hope they will find ways to harvest and use stem cells that reduce the public's ethical concerns about stem-cell research and application.

Stem-cell research and reviving extinct species are two uses for cloning, but there are many more. Molecular cloning basically involves genetic engineering. Scientists can splice DNA fragments and clone the revised DNA into a new cell, which has many applications for medical research, for example. Cells with scientifically engineered recombinant DNA can be cloned and used for disease treatment and gene therapy. If a cell's DNA is engineered to fight a particular disease, and then that cell is cloned and introduced into the body, the theory is that the cells will continue to multiply and effectively fight the disease.

Recombinant DNA can be introduced into animals to help create proteins needed for drug manufacturing too. For example, scientists have been able to introduce into livestock a genetic profile that enables them to produce insulin in their milk. That insulin can then be purified and used by diabetics, who have to inject insulin multiple times a day.

Animals are also purposely cloned with genetic mutations in the name of medical research. Although it sounds harsh to animal lovers, it does contribute to progress in understanding and treating (and, hopefully, eventually curing) certain diseases. For example, medical researchers have long sought a cure for cancer. While there are many treatments (some of them highly effective and able to produce remission in patients), there is currently no simple cure for cancer. When a person gets strep throat, a course of antibiotics cures it. The same cannot be said for cancer—people with cancer face a long, arduous treatment process that may include surgery, radiation, gene therapy, and/or chemotherapy. While some cancers have high cure rates, others do not.

By cloning animals with genetic mutations known to cause certain types of cancer, scientists can produce a greater pool of animals to study in the hopes of finding a cure—or at least a more effective treatment. Regular breeding of animals known to carry the genetic mutation is a possible option, too (and some say a more humane one), but it's a much slower process, and the breeding process can introduce further changes and mutations that make it difficult to create a consistent pool of study subjects.

There are applications beyond human use too. For example, plants with strong survival properties can be cloned to create disease-resistant crops. This has particularly strong potential for third-world countries where citizens face starvation if crop production is negatively impacted.

On the purely whimsical side of things, cloning has also been used to create copies of beloved household pets.

By harvesting and cloning stem cells, scientists might be able to cure different diseases.

It's an expensive process and few people actually do it, but it is an option for people who have tens of thousands of dollars to spare!

Cloning is a fascinating subject with many angles to examine and much progress to be made. Someday we may be living in the world science-fiction authors envisioned when they wrote about cloning years before it happened!

In the 1600s, a plague spread in London because bacteria that cause major disease outbreaks often replicate very fast.

CHAPTER 1

The Problems of Disease, Extinction, and Drug Development

Scientific discovery is generally done to fill a need—that is, scientists see a problem, and they set about trying to discover a solution.

Sometimes, however, there are happy accidents in scientific discovery. For example, in the 1920s, a Scottish biologist named Alexander Fleming was working on investigating staphylococci, a type of bacteria that causes staph infections. He took a vacation, and when he returned to his lab, he discovered a fungus on one of his staph cultures. That fungus appeared to have killed off all the staph bacteria surrounding it. That fungus was eventually developed into the drug penicillin, which is used to treat many bacterial infections and is thought to have saved hundreds of millions of lives since its introduction in 1942.

Fleming's discovery filled a need, but it was a purely accidental discovery. Far more often, scientific discoveries are the results of scientists actively identifying a problem or need and then working to develop a solution. For example, right now there are forms of cancer that are still largely incurable, and scientists are actively working to try to discover the drug or treatment that will change that.

So what problems does cloning solve? Why was it important for scientists to develop this technology? The answer to these questions has many parts.

CLONING for MEDICAL PURPOSES

Although medical science has advanced greatly in the past couple of centuries, there are still many diseases that don't have a cure or an effective treatment—or that have treatments available, but ones with potentially devastating side effects. Not only are scientists working to develop more effective treatments and cures, but they are also working to better understand these diseases and conditions to further inform their work. So, in the medical world, cloning addresses several needs.

Medical Research

Medical research on animal subjects is a controversial topic. Many animal-rights activists say that it's cruel to subject an innocent animal to disease and even death in the name of research. However, the other side of the story is that scientists need some way to learn more about how diseases and conditions work and how treatments can work, and research on lab cultures can take them only so far. At some point, they have to see how a particular disease or condition looks in a living creature, and that's where animals come

While animal testing is inhumane to some, it can be useful to scientists.

into play. (Eventually, human trials are part of development of treatments and the study of diseases and conditions, but not before exhaustive research has been done in the lab and on animal subjects. Human trials are the last stage of the research process.)

When studying diseases and genetic conditions, scientists in modern medical history have genetically engineered animals to create a particular genetic condition or a disease-causing genetic mutation. But this process often requires several generations of breeding, which is time consuming. For some of the diseases scientists are studying and creating these transgenic animals for, time is of the essence. People are still dying from diseases like cancer, and it's in the public's best interests for scientists to develop potential cures as quickly as possible.

This is where cloning can help. Cloning can be done in a single breeding cycle, thereby speeding up the process. In addition, it creates a population of animals that are genetically identical for purposes of testing and study. In multigenerational breeding and creation of transgenic animals, there can be unexpected gene mutations introduced, which may limit the effectiveness of study. Having a genetically identical sample to work with makes research that much more accurate.

Stem Cells

One fairly recent area of study is in the use of stem cells to treat diseases and damaged organs. Stem cells naturally build, maintain, and repair the body during a person's life, and they can be manipulated to work on specific organs and tissues. However, receiving stem cells from a donor isn't necessarily the best treatment option. The body of the person receiving the stem-cell transplant recognizes the stem cells as foreign, which triggers an immune response—in other words, without intervention the body can reject the transferred stem cells.

Scientists are hoping to develop effective ways to clone stem cells from a particular person who needs a stem-cell treatment. That way, the person's body won't reject the cells because they'll be genetically identical to the stem cells already in the person's body. And given stem cells' role in building tissues and organs, there's thought that cloning stem cells might eventually lead to the ability to grow a whole new organ or tissue for a person who needs it. A person with a diseased liver, for example, could potentially receive a transplant of a liver identical to his or her own, grown from the person's very own stem cells. This could greatly reduce the possibility of organ rejection.

Stem cells are showing much promise in treating many diseases and conditions, such as diabetes, Alzheimer's disease, strokes, and spinal cord injuries. Currently, there's a great need to learn as much as possible about stem cells and how they can work to repair the body, and cloning could potentially address that need.

Drug Production

On a similar note, medications to treat diseases and conditions are developed using different proteins. Sometimes these proteins are developed by fermentation in a lab, but that process is slow and costly because it requires huge colonies of cells for the process. Other times, these proteins are purified from their natural (animal) tissue sources, but that process, too, is slow and costly. Also, the purified proteins have the problem of being slightly different from human proteins. For example, insulin to treat diabetes has long been derived from pig or cow insulin, which has a slightly different amino acid sequence than human insulin. This means that some diabetic patients would have an immune response to the pig- or cow-derived insulin.

Cloning human genes is one potential solution to this problem. It eliminates the risk of rejection of substances purified from animal cells.

That's not to say animals don't serve a purpose, though. While cloning human genes addresses the problem of potential rejection, it does not solve the problem of

One application for cloning is repopulating species in decline or reviving extinct species.

mass-producing proteins in an efficient, cost-effective manner. To solve that problem, scientists are looking into genetically modifying animals to produce the needed proteins. For example, cows and goats both produce milk. Scientists can insert a gene that tells the body to produce a particular protein or vaccine into a cow or goat cell, then take the nucleus from the cell and transfer it to a cow or goat egg, as appropriate. That egg would develop into an animal that then carries that particular gene in every cell of its body and thus, would produce milk containing the protein or vaccine. It would also pass that genetic profile on to its offspring, creating more cows or goats that produce the protein or vaccine. If the animals were to be further cloned, scientists could create a genetically identical herd of animals that also produce the protein or vaccine.

Of course, there are some ethical considerations about creating genetically modified animals, but it is one way that scientists have looked to using cloning to address a need in drug development.

CLONING ENDANGERED or EXTINCT SPECIES

The problem of endangered and extinct species is one that environmentalists have long sought to answer. Natural selection is one piece of the equation, of course. Basically, the idea of evolution suggests in part that the species currently inhabiting the earth developed as a result of natural selection, or survival of the fittest. Animals (including humans) developed into the organisms they are now as a means of survival—the species best suited to adapt to their environment continued to populate the earth (and evolve genetically as needed to continue to adapt to the environment). The species not suited to living in the earth's environment gradually died out. So, some extinct species are extinct precisely because they weren't suited to survive on the earth.

Other extinct species are extinct because of external environmental factors. For example, the dinosaurs are thought to have become extinct due to environmental factors. Some people think it was a meteor or asteroid striking the earth, while others believe that strike created a huge amount of dust that threw the earth into darkness for months and created a global cooling. Still others believe that massive volcano eruptions and changes in sea levels and ocean currents caused a change in global climate that dinosaurs were unable to adapt to. But whatever the real cause of the dinosaurs' extinction—and, in reality, it could well be a combination of factors—the end result is that environmental changes caused the dinosaurs to become extinct.

In some cases, extinction isn't really a problem and may indeed be a benefit. One need only read (or watch) *Jurassic Park* to consider one idea about what could happen if dinosaurs were brought back from extinction.

But in other cases, animals are endangered or extinct because of controllable human factors, such as hunting or the destruction of the animal's natural habitat. When animals are rendered endangered or extinct due to such factors, it upsets the natural balance of the environment. The food chain is a good example. Plants and animals are all part of a complex food chain—one organism relies on others for food, and food is necessary for survival. If one part of the food chain

Insulin from pigs has been used to treat diabetes in humans, but there's a chance of an immune reaction to it.

Cloning a Beloved Pet

Given that scientific research has proven that animals can be cloned, some devoted pet owners have expressed the desire to clone their beloved pets. In 2001, a kitten became the first domestic pet ever successfully cloned. Since then, more cats and dogs have been cloned. ViaGen, a Texas company, is one company that will clone pets for a fee. They take DNA from a pet's skin sample and insert it into a donor egg. The resulting embryo is implanted into a surrogate animal, which carries it to term and delivers a healthy cloned animal.

Aside from the ethical concerns that can surround cloning a pet, questions arise about whether the pet will be an exact match and whether the pet will inherit the same diseases or conditions as the original pet. The short answer to these questions is no and not necessarily. The cloned pet will not be an exact match. For example, in a spotted animal, such as a Dalmatian, the cloned pet will still be spotted, but the spot pattern may differ. As for the question about cloned pets inheriting diseases and conditions from the pet from which they were cloned, the answer is not necessarily. If the disease or condition is genetic, then the cloned pet will have the same genetic disease or condition. But if the disease or condition developed

Puppies were cloned in South Korea from a deceased pit bull that belonged to an American woman.

from environmental factors, then the cloned pet would not have that disease.

Personality traits are another variable factor in cloned pets. Personality is determined by nature and nuture. A cloned pet can have different personality traits from the original pet. If the original pet was raised in a healthy environment, it will likely have positive personality traits. The cloned offspring of that pet might have different personality traits depending on how it is raised.

suddenly becomes unavailable or in short supply, it can create a ripple effect of problems up through the food chain.

For example, global warming is causing sea ice to melt. Sea ice is eaten by, among other organisms, zooplankton. Without an adequate supply of sea ice, the zooplankton numbers may dwindle. This may sound like no big deal, but Arctic cod rely on zooplankton for food. If that food supply lessens, the population of Artic cod may be reduced. Seals eat Arctic cod, so without an adequate supply, the number of seals may decline. Finally, seals are a major food source for polar bears, so if the seal population declines, the polar bears may starve and eventually become endangered or extinct. Currently, polar bears are considered a vulnerable species, which means their numbers are dwindling. This is mainly a result of the sea ice habitat melting due to climate change, which, consequently, disrupts the food chain.

The same can happen with plants. If a plant species ceases to exist for any reason—global warming, destruction of habitat, or other reasons—the animals that rely on that plant for nourishment may experience an impact on their population. Further, destruction of plants can impact the earth's atmosphere, further contributing to global warming. So, it's important to address the problem of destruction or depletion of plant species.

While it's unlikely that scientists will attempt to resurrect the dinosaurs—even if they wanted to, it would be a nearly impossible task since it would be difficult to find a well-preserved DNA source for the dinosaurs—cloning can be (and is being) used to attempt to resurrect other endangered and extinct species whose repopulation and reintroduction could potentially provide environmental benefit to the earth.

CLONING LIVESTOCK

As mentioned earlier, livestock may be cloned for the purposes of creating animals that can produce proteins used in drug development. However, there is another reason why livestock may be cloned: to produce a strong herd of animals. Sometimes disease can wipe out livestock. This creates food shortages or an imbalance of livestock use in farming and agriculture and potentially affects humans.

For example, from 1986 through 2001, an epidemic of mad cow disease swept through the United Kingdom, affecting approximately 180,000 cattle. This devastated the United Kingdom's farming communities and their economy of exporting beef, especially when it was found that consuming meat or other products from a cow with mad cow disease could lead people to develop variant Creutzfeldt-Jakob disease, a fatal brain disease. (Milk from affected cows reportedly did *not* transmit the disease. But eating the meat or other products from the animal did.) The impact of the mad cow disease outbreak was global. There were cows affected in Canada and the United States, although the majority of cases were in the United Kingdom. At the height of the outbreak, numerous countries banned the import of meat from the United Kingdom, which affected the United Kingdom's economy.

Problems like this one can be addressed by the practice of cloning livestock. In theory, as long as scientists carefully identify which animals are the healthiest and strongest, they can clone a superior herd of livestock. They don't intend to clone all livestock that will be consumed—a process that would be far too expensive and time consuming. But if they clone a superior herd of livestock, that herd can then reproduce naturally, providing a good source of livestock.

CLONING HUMANS

In general terms, human cloning is not on the horizon. Scientists are not looking to clone humans to create a genetically superior—and identical—race of people, as some science-fiction tales might suggest. For one thing, animal cloning is not universally successful. There are many instances in which a cloned embryo does not develop properly or is not successfully carried to term by the surrogate mother. It largely depends on the animal species. Cats and mice are relatively easy to successfully clone, but dogs and rats are harder. Primates are quite difficult to successfully clone.

But more pressing are the ethical concerns that come along with human cloning. Even if scientists could develop an effective process for cloning humans, there are still ethical barriers. Cloning borders very closely on eugenics. People wouldn't seek to clone an individual with undesirable traits or with undesirable genetic conditions, which means human cloning would likely stray into the territory of creating what some might deem as genetically superior people. It would potentially eliminate diversity in human society, which many people feel is a dangerous road to go down.

On a purely commercial level, too, there is no market for cloning. The ethical concerns have resulted in the medical and pharmaceutical communities declaring that they have no interest in human cloning. Even though it could solve issues of infertility for some couples wanting to have children, it's not a path the medical community wants to take because of the ethical concerns.

The cold reality is that many scientific endeavors are driven by profit. Drug companies invest in creating new drugs to help people but also because developing new drugs to help people results in a profit for them. Assisted reproduction companies help couples conceive children to help them but also because it yields a profit. So, when these communities say they have no interest in supporting human cloning and using that technology, there is no profit motive for scientists to work on developing human cloning.

For these reasons, although human cloning could happen, it's not terribly likely. The exception, of course, is cloning embryonic stem cells, which shows much promise in treating diseases and conditions. For some people, there are ethical concerns with this as well. An embryo, to them, is technically a human life, and thus, should not be used solely for the purposes of science. But to others, an embryo is not yet a life, but rather a *potential* life, and thus, it is not ethically concerning to use that embryo for the good of science and medicine.

To address all of these problems and concerns, scientists have developed cloning technologies that have led to major strides in medical research and drug development.

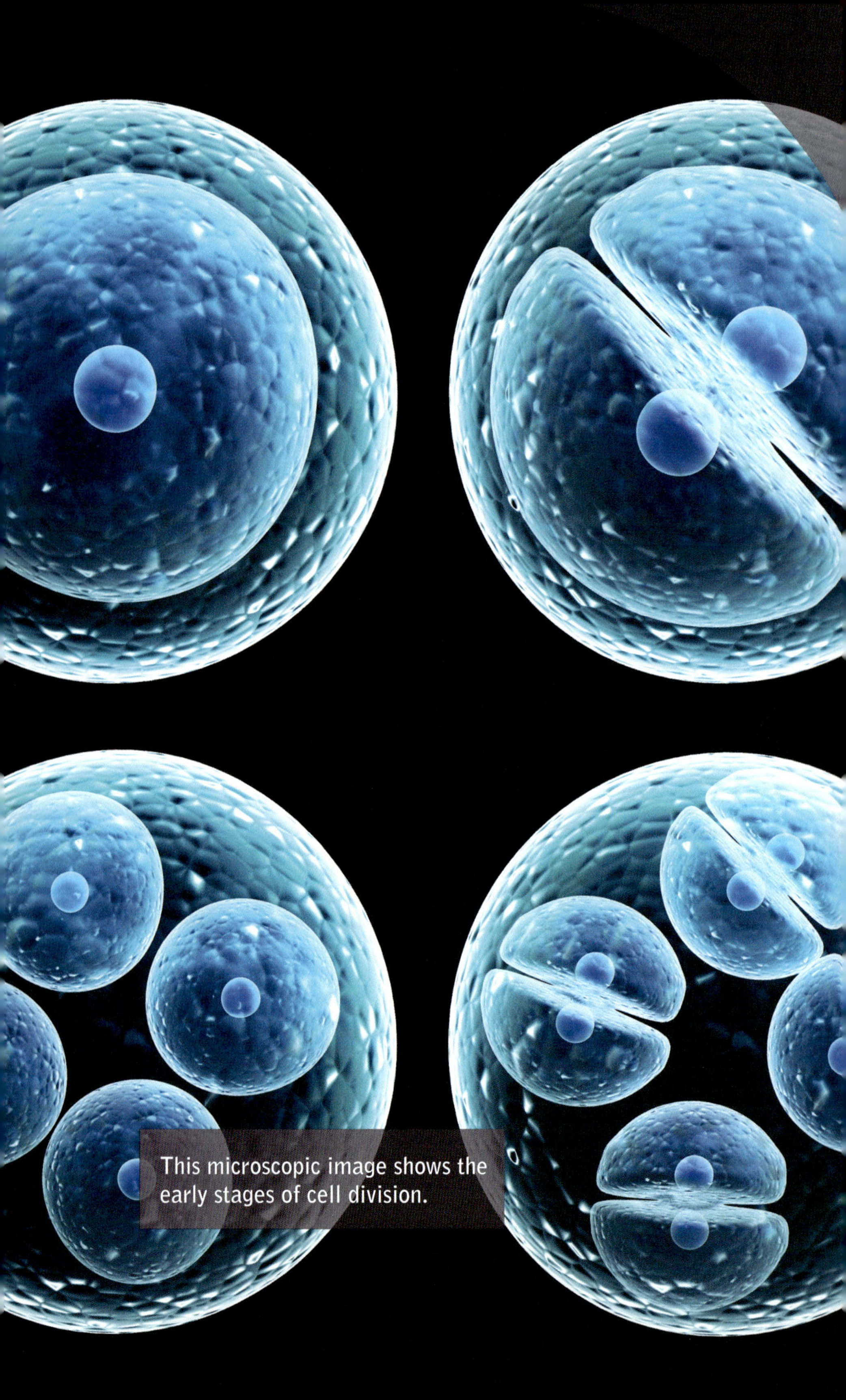

This microscopic image shows the early stages of cell division.

CHAPTER 2

The Science of Cloning

Scientific discovery is based on questions, hypotheses, previous knowledge, and imitation, among other factors. In a business, employees may hold brainstorming sessions to come up with new ideas and solutions to problems. What one person says may inspire someone else in the group to come up with another idea.

In the world of science, it's not so different. Scientists see a problem, and when considering how to address or answer it, they often look to established science and build upon it to inform their own discovery. For example, Gregor Mendel's work with pea plants is considered one of the building blocks in the field of genetics, but many scientists after him have considered his work and built upon it with new discoveries of their own. Barbara McClintock, for example, was informed by Mendel's work when she made her groundbreaking discoveries about genetic recombination while working with maize.

The science of cloning is no exception. When the study of cloning began, scientists first had to understand asexual reproduction and the ways that different structures can replicate themselves—or can lend themselves to manual replication.

ASEXUAL REPRODUCTION

In the most natural sense, cloning is asexual reproduction. Humans and most other vertebrates reproduce sexually. Their reproduction involves the union of gametes, or reproductive cells, which fuse and combine their chromosomes to give their offspring's cells chromosomes from both the female and the male. Sexual reproduction involves two "parents"—a male and a female. Each contributes half of the chromosomes needed for the offspring's cells.

Asexual reproduction, on the other hand, occurs when an organism can reproduce on its own. There is no need for two gametes to fuse, and the number of chromosomes in the offspring almost always remains the same as in the parent. Single-celled organisms such as bacteria and archaea reproduce asexually, as do all prokaryotes and many types of plants and fungi. Some eukaryotes reproduce asexually, but some reproduce sexually.

There are many different types of asexual reproduction, including binary fission, budding, vegetative propagation, sporogenesis, fragmentation, parthenogenesis, apomixis, and nucellar embryony.

In binary fission, which is the method of asexual reproduction for archaea, bacteria, and protists, the cell divides into two smaller cells, which can then grow to the size of the original cell. The cell starts the process

Asexual reproduction is taking place on the edge of this leaf.

by replicating its genetic material, then it segregates the chromosomes to opposite sides of the cell, and finally the cytoplasm and plasma membrane split into two genetically identical cells.

In budding, an organism, such as a plant, a fungus, a virus, or an embryo, forms an outgrowth, or bud, that is genetically identical to the main body of the organism. Sometimes the bud remains attached to the original organism, and sometimes it detaches and becomes a separate organism. Either way, it remains a clone of the initial organism.

Some plants can be cloned through vegetative propagation. In this process, a specialized part of the plant (usually a stem, leaf, or root) can take root and grow a clone of the original plant. Horticulturists sometimes manually propagate plants. But, the process can also occur naturally, such as when a plant naturally sheds a leaf or stem that then naturally takes root in the soil and begins to grow a new plant.

Sporogenesis refers to the production of spores, which is a method of asexual reproduction that occurs in some eukaryotic organisms such as plants, algae, and fungi. Spores are generally formed during cell division (during either meiosis or mitosis), though sometimes they form during cell fusion.

Fragmentation occurs when an organism breaks apart into fragments, which can then grow into genetically identical new organisms. Organisms that use this method of asexual reproduction include sea stars, annelid worms, and some fungi and plants.

Parthenogenesis shares a similarity with sexual reproduction in that it involves a female gamete. However, in sexual reproduction a female gamete must be fertilized by a male gamete for reproduction to occur. In parthenogenesis, this is not the case. The female gamete can develop into a genetically identical offspring without fertilization from a male gamete. Parthenogenesis is a fairly common form of asexual reproduction that is used by plants; some invertebrates, such as aphids, certain ants, bees, and parasitic wasps; and some vertebrates, such as certain reptiles, amphibians, fish, and birds.

There are two types of parthenogenesis: apomictic and automictic. Apomictic parthenogenesis results in offspring that are genetically identical to the mother organism, with the exact same number of chromosomes. Automictic parthenogenesis results in offspring with only half of the mother's chromosomes.

Apomictic parthenogenesis is one type of apomictic reproduction. But "apomixis" is also a more general term used to describe any asexual reproduction that doesn't involve fertilization and meiosis (separation of chromosomes during cell division). Apomixis commonly occurs in plants, including certain flowering plants.

Another type of apomixis, in addition to apomictic parthenogenesis, is nucellar embryony. This method of seed reproduction takes place in many varieties of citrus and certain other plant species. In this type of asexual reproduction, embryos that are genetically identical to the parent plant are created.

If cloning of unicellular and multicellular organisms was occurring naturally in many species, scientists needed only to understand the process in order to form their own hypotheses about manually cloning molecules, cells, or organisms—or about how these cloned structures and organisms might be useful in further scientific study in related areas, such as immunology and pathology.

MOLECULAR CLONING

The form of cloning that works on the most microscopic level is molecular cloning. In this type of cloning, molecules, which are the smallest units of chemical compounds, made up of groups of atoms bonded together, are replicated exactly. Often, molecular cloning is used to recreate fragments of DNA.

But before scientists could even begin to learn how to recreate molecules such as fragments of DNA, they needed to understand how DNA works and how cells replicate.

The acronym DNA stands for deoxyribonucleic acid, which describes the hereditary material in nearly all organisms. In other words, DNA is the blueprint of an organism. It's the genetic code that sketches out everything about an organism. In humans and animals, each organism's DNA is unique. The whole of an organism's genetic material is called a genome, and the genome is made up of a double helix of DNA that involves pairs of chemical bases attached to a sugar-phosphate backbone. Strands of DNA look a bit like a spiral ladder, with the rungs made up of pairs of chemical bases.

The base pairs are made up of four chemical bases: adenine, guanine, cytosine, and thymine. Adenine and thymine pair together, and guanine and cytosine pair

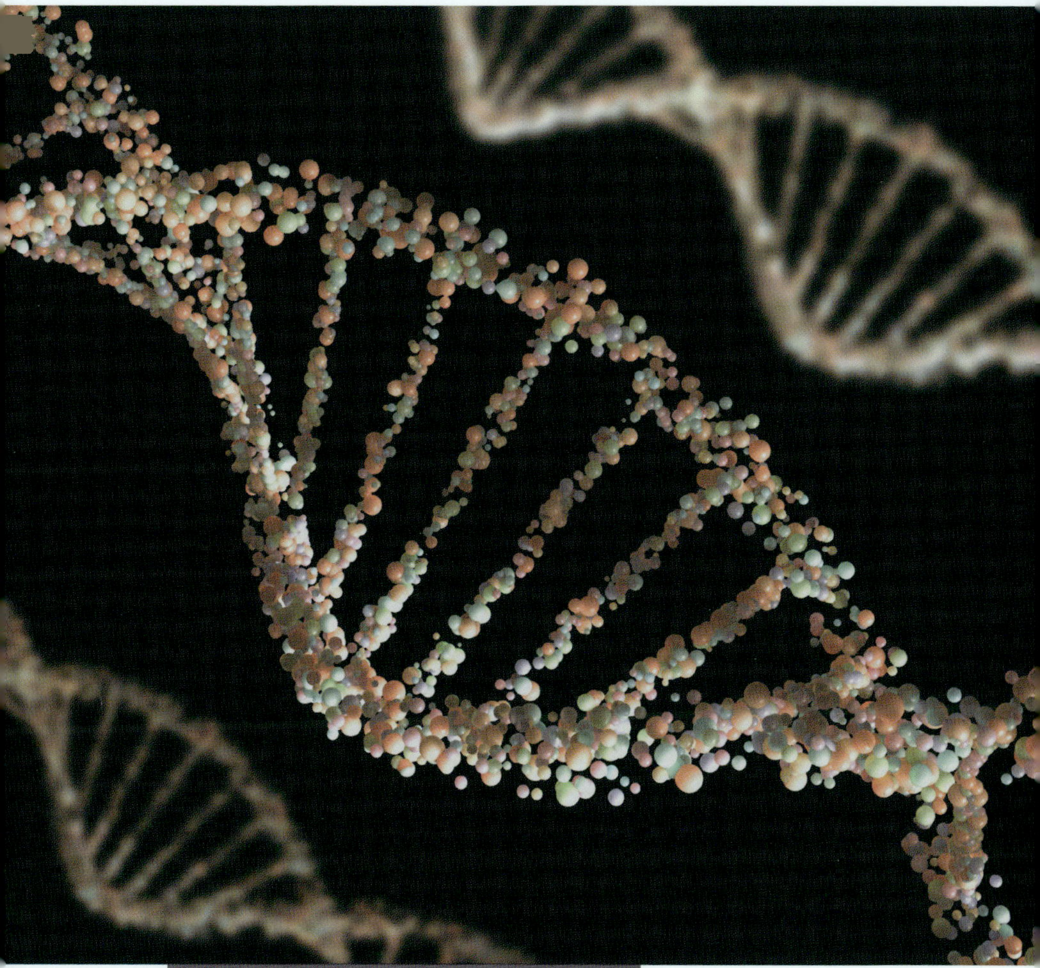

DNA, the blueprint of an organism, has a double-helix structure that looks like a spiral ladder.

together to make up the rungs of the double-helix ladder. The order in which those rungs are arranged determines the genetic code of the individual. A good analogy is how letters make up words. The English alphabet has twenty-six letters that can be combined in innumerable ways to make up different words. No two unique words have the same letters arranged in the exact same order. Human DNA is the same. No two humans will have the same sequence of chemical pairs in the same order in their DNA. The exception is identical twins, which we will explore a little later.

Human DNA has about three billion bases, so the order in which those pairs are arranged in the double helix is different for every individual. It would be virtually impossible for two people to have the same genetic code, given the number of possibilities, especially since chromosomes, which carry DNA, can have genetic variations in the form of microdeletions and duplications, which are considered gene mutations.

The exception to this rule is identical twins. Identical twins occur when a single fertilized egg splits into two shortly after fertilization. That results in two embryos with identical DNA growing in a mother's body. These embryos then develop into two fetuses with identical DNA. When the babies are born, they still have identical DNA—that never changes. However, small variations may be evident in identical twins due to environmental and epigenetic factors.

Sometimes chemical changes occur in DNA as an organism grows, which can account for the very slight variations sometimes seen in identical twins. However, the twins' DNA is still ultimately the same because the basic structure of an organism's DNA never changes throughout its lifespan.

Plants are an exception to the rule too. Sexually reproducing organisms, such as humans and most animals, get their DNA from both a female and a male parent. But plants can be sexually reproducing or asexually reproducing. If they're sexually reproducing, no two plants will have the same DNA. But if they're asexually reproducing, their form of reproduction is a form of cloning, and then two plants will have the same DNA unless some sort of genetic mutation occurs.

Scientists gained a far greater understanding of DNA in 1953, when scientists James Watson and Francis Crick identified the double-helix structure of DNA. However, that is not when DNA was actually discovered. That process began far earlier, in the 1860s, when Swiss chemist Johann Friedrich Miescher unexpectedly stumbled upon DNA while researching the components of white blood cells. Miescher referred to his finding as "nuclein" because he thought it came from the cell nucleus, but we now know that what Miescher found was DNA. Because no one had ever identified the substance before, and Miescher had no previous work to rely on, it was difficult for him to convey to the scientific community what he had found and what it meant. But in the early 1880s, German biochemist Albrecht Kossel continued Miescher's work and classified nuclein as a nucleic acid. He also gave it its name: deoxyribonucleic acid. Further, Kossel is credited with identifying the building blocks of DNA and RNA (another nucleic acid present in all cells): adenine, cytosine, guanine, thymine, and uracil (found in RNA but not DNA—uracil takes the place of thymine in RNA). In 1910, Kossel was awarded the Nobel Prize in Physiology or Medicine for his groundbreaking work on DNA and RNA.

By understanding the function of DNA and how molecules replicate, scientists could begin to consider how cloning molecules might be possible in a laboratory setting or as a means of furthering scientific development in fields such as immunology, virology, and pathology.

CELL CLONING

The next type of cloning is cell cloning. Molecules are parts of cells. A cell is made up of many molecules. If you look at the building of organisms as a staircase, the very bottom step is atoms. The second step is molecules. Atoms make up molecules, which engage in replication and cloning. The third step is cells, which are made up of molecules. Cells, in turn, combine to make up the fourth step—tissues. Tissues work together to make up the fifth step, organs. Organs work together in organ systems, and all of the organ systems in a body make up the entire organism—the final step.

Scientists studying cloning at the most minute level work on molecules, and scientists studying cloning at a slightly less minute level work on cells.

To begin to consider the idea of cell cloning, scientists had to understand how chromosomes contribute to the reproductive process. Chromosomes are string-like structures present in cells. They are made up of a DNA molecule wrapped around a protein. Different species of plants and animals have different numbers of chromosomes.

Humans generally have twenty-three pairs of chromosomes, but in certain genetic conditions this can be different. For example, in Down syndrome, or trisomy 21, the individual has a third twenty-first chromosome. This is most often present in every cell in a person with Down syndrome, though there is a rare form called mosaic Down syndrome in which the third twenty-first chromosome is present only in some cells. Even bacteria have chromosomes, but they are often loops or circles of DNA, rather than the standard double-helix seen in most organisms.

In the mid-1800s, a German anatomist named Walther Flemming discovered what we now call chromosomes in

MITOSIS

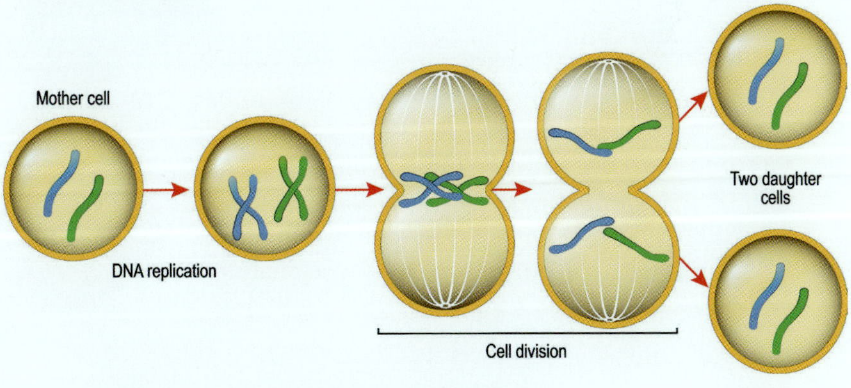

In mitosis, a parent cell's DNA replicates, and then the cell divides into two daughter cells.

Gregor Mendel: The Father of Genetics

In the late 1800s, scientists learned that genetic material parents pass to their offspring is contained on chromosomes. But they were building off the discovery of an earlier scientist, an Austrian friar named Gregor Johann Mendel. Scientists had long known that animals and plants could both be crossbred to attempt to produce offspring with desirable traits, but Mendel's work established what are now known as the laws of Mendelian inheritance.

Mendel worked with crossbreeding pea plants and studied numerous characteristics of the parent plants and their offspring: plant height, flower position and color, seed shape and color, and pod shape and color. In studying how these various characteristics appeared in the offspring of the pea plants he crossbred, Mendel produced a theory of dominant and recessive genes. For example, he noted that pea plants had either white or purple flowers, and if he crossbred one of each plant, they didn't result in a plant with blended flowers in a light purple or lavender shade. Instead, they generally produced a plant with purple flowers, but occasionally a plant with white flowers resulted. The reason for this was that white flowers resulted from a recessive gene that would only be expressed if it combined with another recessive gene for a white flower. If a dominant gene for purple flowers was present, it would overpower the recessive gene for white flowers, and the resulting plant would have purple flowers. This theory became known as the law of dominance.

Mendel also established the law of segregation, in which he stated that for organisms that reproduce sexually (and thus have gametes), alleles (genes) for each trait separate during meiosis, which means the resulting gamete has only one allele for a given trait, instead of the usual two. Because offspring result from two gametes joining, the offspring would get one allele for a specific trait from the male parent and the second allele for a specific trait from the female parent. Mendel also determined the law of independent assortment, which established that the selection of one allele for a trait does not in any way influence the selection of another allele for another trait.

the nucleus of cells. He also identified how chromosomes separate during mitosis, or cell division. Like most scientists, Flemming was working off amassed knowledge in the field of science. So, even though he is often credited with discovering mitosis, other scientists, including botanist Hugo von Mohl and zoologist Otto Bütschli, were also exploring how cells replicate and divide.

Mitosis is generally how eukaryotic cells divide. Mitosis results in cloned cells—the cells formed from the original cell are genetically identical. Prokaryotic cells do not have a nucleus, so they divide by binary fission instead.

Mitosis varies somewhat between plant and animal cells. Mitosis in animal cells consists of four main phases: prophase, metaphase, anaphase, and telophase. Some scientists further define other stages of mitosis, but in general, the process has these four main phases. Before the first phase, prophase, the DNA replicates within the cell. (Some scientists refer to this as interphase.) In prophase, the nuclear membrane breaks down and chromatin condenses into chromosomes that are grouped together in pairs. The centrioles, which at that point are near the nucleus, move to opposite sides of the cell, and a spindle made of fibers and microtubules begins to form between them.

The next stage is metaphase. In this stage, spindle fibers attach to the centromere of each pair of chromosomes. The chromosomes line up in the center of the cell, which is known as the equator.

Next comes anaphase, in which the spindle fibers shorten to break apart the pairs of chromosomes and their centromeres. One piece of each chromosome pair, known as a chromatid, moves to each end (or pole) of the cell, which

Sea sponges are unique in that they can reproduce either asexually or sexually.

results in each pole of the cell having a complete set of chromosomes when anaphase is complete.

Finally, in telophase, the chromosomes form chromatin, the spindle breaks down, and two new nuclear membranes form.

Cytokinesis, which some scientists consider part of mitosis, is where the cell actually divides. The cytoplasm of the cell splits, and two new, identical cells form. Cytokinesis happens in both eukaryotes and prokaryotes, and mitosis is strictly a process for eukaryotes, which may explain why most scientists consider cytokinesis separate from the process of mitosis, rather than as a final stage of it.

Working off Flemming's discoveries, Walter Sutton and Theodor Boveri (working on separate research in the late 1800s) determined that the genetic material parents pass down to their offspring is contained on chromosomes.

ORGANISM CLONING

Once scientists had a basic understanding of DNA, genetics, and cell division, they could begin to consider cloning in more depth. They knew that if organisms could clone cells naturally, understanding that process and potentially replicating it in a lab setting could provide the basis for major scientific breakthroughs.

Organisms are at the top of the body staircase, so to speak. Cloning an organism such as a person might seem like the stuff of science fiction, but many organisms aren't nearly as complex as a human body and thus can clone themselves (or, in theory, be cloned by scientists). For example, bacteria, some insects, some plants, and some animals reproduce asexually and thus already clone themselves. Sea sponges clone themselves, as do tapeworms and aphids. Some reptiles are even able to clone themselves, including whiptail lizards and komodo dragons. There is even a recorded case of a hammerhead shark cloning herself through parthenogenesis in 2001.

Mammals, however, cannot reproduce asexually, and thus, they cannot spontaneously clone themselves. That hasn't stopped scientists from wondering about cloning mammals, though, and even attempting to do so. In 1996, Dolly the sheep became the first mammal successfully cloned from a cell from an adult mammal. Frogs, mice, and cows had already been cloned in labs, but they had been cloned from DNA taken from animal embryos. Dolly was the first to be cloned from an adult cell.

But before scientists could even attempt to clone a mammal, they had to fully understand how the molecules, cells, tissues, organs, and organ systems of that mammal worked together to form an organism and how mammals reproduce. Reproduction has been studied for centuries, so scientists working in the mid- to late twentieth century certainly had plenty of scientific basis to go on. But a true understanding of genetics and cytology was still evolving. (Science is always evolving, but cytology and genetics are relatively new topics in the grand scheme of biology and life science.) For example, Barbara McClintock's groundbreaking research on genetic recombination in plant cells took place in the mid-twentieth century, but it was largely ignored until the late 1970s and early 1980s (when she eventually won a Nobel Prize for her work).

Scientists in the 1980s knew that in mammals, fertilized cells reproduce to create an embryo. They also knew that as cell division and development of organs continues, the embryo becomes a fetus and, eventually, is born as offspring to the parents. So, the first successful attempt at cloning a mammal occurred in 1984, when scientists captured one cell from an eight-cell embryo and fused it to an egg cell. The new cell began dividing and ultimately developed into the first cloned mammal.

Even that landmark discovery, though, was a building block for animal cloning on a larger scale. Cloning from an already developing embryo was one thing, but cloning from an adult cell was another. Adult cells in mammals typically shut down genes they no longer need (whereas all genes can be activated in an embryo). So, cloning an animal when an embryo wasn't present to use required further scientific experimentation and discovery. Scientists had to learn how to reactivate dormant genes.

A CYCLE of INFORMATION and DISCOVERY

Science is a field where knowledge and discovery build upon themselves and inform other knowledge and discovery. Such is the case with genetics, reproduction, and cloning. As scientists learned more about reproduction, they also learned more about genetics and how genetic information is passed from a parent organism to its offspring. Their discoveries in genetics in turn informed their knowledge about reproduction. For example, as genetics has evolved, the science of infertility and reproductive assistance has evolved as well. Further, as scientists have learned more about genetics, it has informed their work in the study of cloning.

Studies of anatomy, physiology, botany, and more have also informed the current research being done on cloning. To successfully clone an organism, scientists must know exactly how that organism works and how all of its organ systems are composed and work together. As the study of cloning and asexual reproduction has continued, we understand more about how animal and plant structures and systems develop.

Through an endless cycle of research, hypothesis, discovery, and information, we gain a better understanding of the world around us. This knowledge is used to develop new technology and medicines that improve our lives. Great discoveries in science don't happen without the discoveries of the past. We will now explore the important figures who shaped our understanding of cloning.

Nobel Prize winner Hans Spemann developed a procedure for splitting cells using hair.

CHAPTER 3

The Major Players in the World of Cloning

Like most major scientific discoveries, the science of cloning wasn't discovered overnight. It also wasn't discovered solely by one scientist or team of scientists. Many scientists over a long period of time made discoveries in the field that ultimately contributed to our current body of scientific knowledge about cloning. While it would be impossible to discuss every person who contributed to the body of knowledge about the science of cloning, this chapter will discuss some of the key players.

STARTING with a SEA URCHIN

The first successfully cloned animal was a relatively simple species: the sea urchin. The cloning can be credited to Hans Adolf Eduard Driesch, a German biologist with a strong interest in zoology and embryology. In 1891, Driesch discovered that by shaking a two-celled sea urchin embryo, he could separate the two cells. Those two cells could then grow separately into two complete sea urchins.

The sea urchin was the first animal to be successfully cloned.

This provided evidence that each cell contains the complete genetic information for a sea urchin. It is in stark contrast to the assertion by Wilhelm Roux, a German zoologist and embryologist who had just a few years earlier suggested that different embryonic cells from the same organism had different functions and thus contained different genetic material.

Driesch also made other discoveries that were important to cytology and genetics. One of his experiments proved that all nuclei are equivalent in all cells from an embryo. He also discovered how the nucleus and cytoplasm of a cell interact and how embryonic cells interact with one another.

MOVING on to SALAMANDERS

Sea urchins are relatively simple organisms. A few years after Driesch's experiments, another German embryologist, Hans Spemann, carried on with further experiments in cloning. Spemann was working on salamanders, whose embryonic cells were more difficult to separate than those of the relatively simple sea urchin. In 1902, Spemann got the idea to split the cells with a hair. He created a tiny noose from baby hair and tightened it between two embryonic cells from a salamander until it essentially "cut" the cells apart. The split cells did indeed form into two separate but identical salamanders, just as the sea urchins in Driesch's experiment had done. However, Spemann found that this technique worked only up until a certain early stage of embryonic development. When he tried to split the cells of embryos later in the development process, the experiments weren't nearly as successful, and the salamanders weren't as likely to develop into adults. Unlike sea urchins, salamanders are vertebrates, which made Spemann's experiments particularly noteworthy because they marked the first time a scientist had cloned a vertebrate.

Spemann continued his work with salamanders, and in 1928, he made another notable contribution to the field of cloning. This time, Spemann used a baby-hair noose to squeeze (not split) a fertilized salamander egg. Because the egg has only one nucleus, this resulted in the nucleus being pushed to one side of the egg's cytoplasm. Spemann left the tightened noose on and watched what happened.

The side of the egg with the nucleus divided into more cells, just as a fertilized egg normally would. The side of the egg without the nucleus, on the other hand, remained static and did not divide.

When the side with the nucleus had divided into sixteen cells, Spemann loosened the noose, which let the nucleus slide back into the other side of the egg. He then retightened the noose to "cut" the original cell into two, leaving one separate cell and one cell with sixteen replicated cells attached. All of the cells, including the lone one, developed into salamander embryos.

This is the first known instance of successful nuclear transfer and showed that the nucleus directs the growth of the salamander.

MOVING on to FROGS

In the 1950s, American scientists Robert Briggs and Thomas King, working at the Lankenau Institute for Medical Research in Wynnewood, Pennsylvania, continued Spemann's work on nuclear transfer. However, their approach differed slightly, as did their subject.

Working on frogs, Briggs and King took the nucleus out of a cell in an early-stage tadpole embryo and transferred it into a frog egg from which they had removed the nucleus. They were curious whether a full nuclear transfer would be successful, and indeed it was successful. The cell the nucleus was transferred into developed into a tadpole.

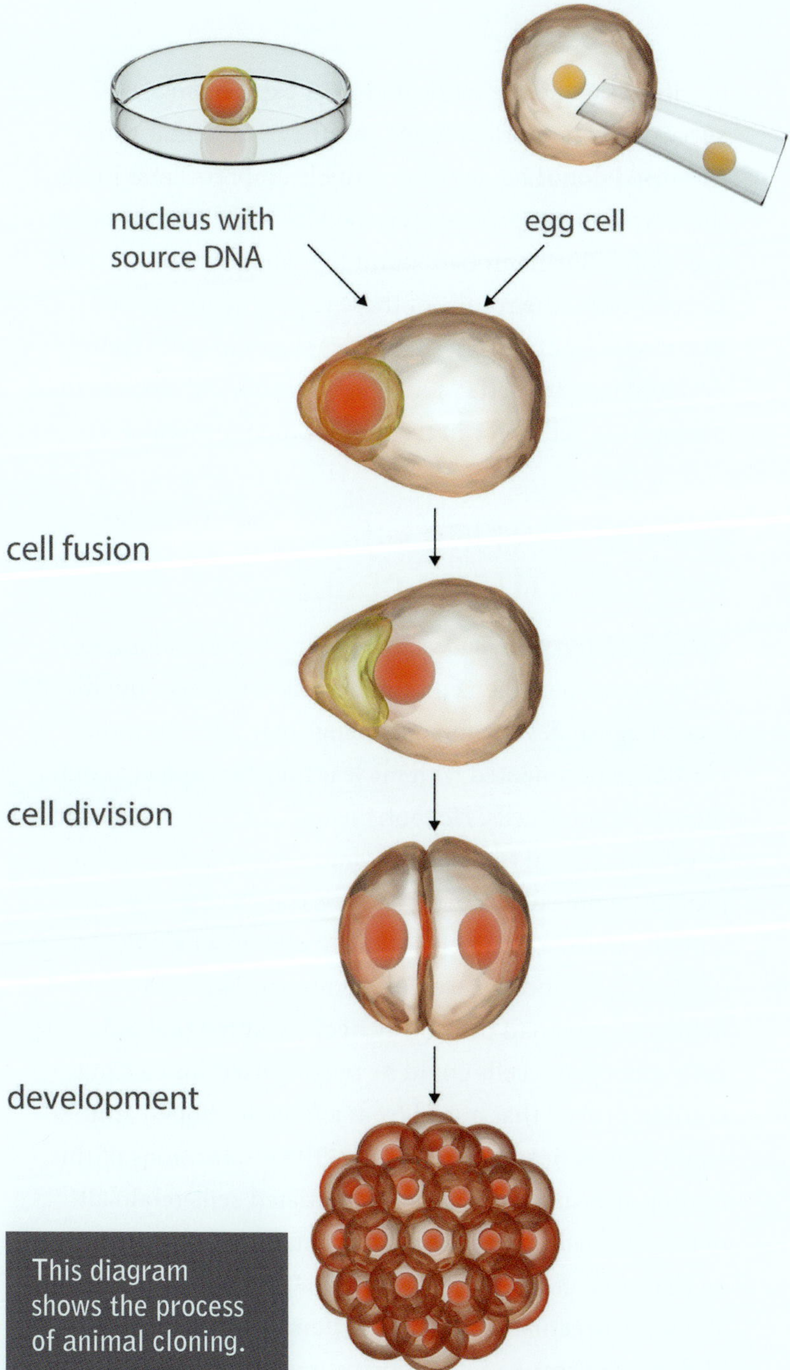

This diagram shows the process of animal cloning.

Briggs and King replicated their experiments successfully numerous times, but they found that when they used donor nuclei from tadpole embryos later in the development process, the transfer wasn't nearly as successful. Spemann had found the same in his work with salamanders. The results of these experiments showed that nuclei from cells in the earlier stages of embryonic development are better suited for transfer and cloning than nuclei from cells later in the development process.

EXPERIMENTING with DIFFERENTIATED CELLS

Up to the late 1950s, successful cloning experiments had been carried out when embryonic cells were used. But in 1958, English developmental biologist Sir John Bertrand Gurdon experimented with nuclear transfer from cells other than embryonic cells. He took the nucleus from a tadpole's intestinal cell and transferred it into a frog egg that had its nucleus removed. His experiment was a success. The egg with the transferred nucleus developed into a tadpole.

Gurdon's findings were incredibly important to the field because it had previously been assumed that only early embryonic cells could be reliably used for cloning. Gurdon proved that nuclei from a fully developed animal could indeed be used for cloning. The implications of this finding also suggested that differentiated cells retain all of the organism's genetic information. In other words, an intestinal cell doesn't just contain genetic information about the organism's digestive system; rather, it contains all of the organism's genetic information.

The first attempts to clone mammals were done using cells from rabbits.

Some scientists thought that perhaps the intestinal cell Gurdon used was actually a stem cell, which would indeed contain all of the genetic information. However, later experiments performed by scientists in Switzerland in the mid-1970s proved Gurdon's claim that differentiated cells contain all of an organism's genetic information. That group used nuclei they could prove were fully differentiated, and they were successful in cloning tadpoles.

MOVING on to MAMMAL EMBRYOS

Although sea urchins, salamanders, and tadpoles are small organisms, their cells are actually large compared to the egg cells of mammals. So, scientists could work on them even without the advanced microscopy tools scientists have access to today.

In 1975, with decidedly more advanced technology than Spemann's baby-hair noose, English scientist J. Derek Bromhall experimented with the cells of rabbit embryos. He used a glass pipette as a tiny straw and "sucked" the nucleus from the cell of a rabbit embryo. He then transferred the nucleus into a rabbit egg cell that had its nucleus removed. After a few days, the cell had divided and a more advanced embryo had formed.

Bromhall's work showed that nuclear transfer could successfully clone mammal embryos. However, Bromhall did not take his experiment far enough to determine whether the embryo would have developed into an actual rabbit. He did not transfer the more advanced embryo into the womb of a mother rabbit to see whether it would continue to grow, develop, and eventually be born.

SUCCESS with MAMMAL CLONING

In 1984, Danish scientist Steen Malte Willadsen took Bromhall's experiment a step further and became the first person to successfully clone a mammal (not just a mammal embryo) by the process of nuclear transfer.

In his experiment, Willadsen removed one cell from an eight-cell lamb embryo. He then fused that cell to an egg cell that had the nucleus removed. The process worked, and the cell began dividing into a more developed embryo. Willadsen put the lamb embryos into the womb of a mother sheep and waited to see whether a successful birth would result. It did, and three live lambs were born to the surrogate mother sheep.

In essence, Willadsen was mimicking in vitro fertilization, a fertility treatment being successfully used in humans by this point. The difference was, human embryos implanted in a mother's womb were the result of a sperm fertilizing an egg, just as happens during normal conception except with the in vitro technique, the fertilization was done manually, outside the body, and then the fertilized egg was implanted. There was no cloning done in human in vitro treatment, whereas Willadsen's experiment was designed as a further test of the possibilities of cloning.

Three years later, in 1987, American scientists Neal First, Randal Prather, and Willard Eyestone used a process similar to Willadsen's experiment and successfully cloned two calves, proving that sheep were not the only mammals that could be successfully cloned by nuclear transfer from embryonic cells.

FURTHER EXPERIMENTATION with NUCLEAR TRANSFER

Most cloning experiments up until the mid-1990s had used nuclear transfer from embryonic cells early in the development process. John Gurdon's experiments with frogs in the late 1950s showed that somatic cells—nonreproductive cells—could be used successfully for nuclear transfer, but his experimentation was limited to frogs. In 1996, British embryologist Ian Wilmut and British biologist Keith Campbell experimented with transferring donor nuclei from cells cultured in a laboratory.

Like Steen Willadsen, Wilmut and Campbell worked with sheep cells. They transferred nuclei from the cultured cells into sheep eggs that had their nuclei removed, and the result was the successful birth of two lambs.

Hello Dolly

Wilmut and Campbell continued their experimentation that same year with the first successful cloning of a mammal through somatic cell nuclear transfer. The mammal in question was a sheep named Dolly, and her birth grabbed headlines worldwide.

Building on their success in cloning a mammal from lab-cultured cells and Gurdon's work on using somatic cells of frogs to successfully clone tadpoles, Wilmut and Campbell took nuclei from udder cells from adult sheep and transferred them into eggs that had their nuclei removed. They did 277 transfers, and only one resulted in an embryo that was ultimately carried to term and born to a surrogate mother sheep. Still, that one success was enough to prove that mammals could be cloned from differentiated somatic cells—that is, they didn't have to be cloned from embryonic cells.

Hello Polly

Wilmut and Campbell's experiment was important because it tied into other scientific research being done on cells. Scientists had developed methods to transfer specific genes into lab-cultured cells, so the fact that cultured cells could result in a successful live birth suggested that perhaps modified cells could someday be used to create transgenic animals that could be used for advances in fields such as medicine. For example, scientists theorized that perhaps this technology could lead to cows that could produce insulin for diabetics in their milk.

Wilmut and Campbell continued their experimentation in this vein by collaborating with German scientist and professor Angelika Schnieke, who had worked on manufacturing pharmaceutical products in the milk of livestock. The team grew sheep skin cells in the lab and then introduced the human Factor IX gene into those cultured cells. Factor IX contains the genetic code for a protein that helps human blood clot; it is used as a treatment for hemophiliacs who are unable to successfully form blood clots.

Once they had cultured cells that contained Factor IX in them, the team transferred the nuclei from these cells into sheep egg cells that had the nucleus removed and transferred the resulting embryo into a surrogate mother sheep. The

Dolly and the Ethics of Cloning

Normally, sheep aren't the sort of animal that spark a lot of debate. But Dolly was different. Because of how Dolly was created, she became a household topic of debate. In response to Dolly's birth, some countries preemptively banned human cloning and established jail terms or other significant punishments for anyone who attempted to try it. Even Dr. Wilmut, the scientist who led the group that created Dolly, recognized the potential problems with cloning: "We believe that it is important that society decides how we want to use this technology and makes sure it prohibits what it wants to prohibit. It would be desperately sad if people started using this sort of technology with people."

Sheep are mammals, and the scientific advances demonstrated by Dolly's successful birth made people question whether the same could be done with humans, who are also mammals. The fact that human cloning might now be possible was enough to worry many people. For some people, creating a child by cloning is "playing God." Even people who aren't necessarily religious question whether it's wise to interrupt the natural order of things. Critics of this argument, though, point to assisted

The famous cloned sheep Dolly is shown here at about seven months old.

reproductive technology (ART). Fertility treatments, which are widely accepted by a great portion of the population, are also interfering with the natural process of reproduction, so they ask where the line should be drawn. Other critics of cloning worry about eugenics and the idea that society would become less diverse if people were able to clone donors with certain desirable traits. But opponents of this argument suggest that in some ways this can already happen. Parents seeking help with fertility problems can use a process where eggs are fertilized outside of the womb and then tested to see whether they have certain genetic conditions. The eggs found to have genetic abnormalities are then discarded.

Scientists have barely ventured into the world of human cloning. However, all it took was one cloned sheep to incite a flurry of debate.

In 2009, scientists successfully cloned an extinct mountain goat known as the bucardo, but the animal did not live long.

mother sheep gave birth to Polly, a lamb who was able to produce milk that contained the Factor IX protein.

This was a huge development in cloning science because it was evidence that cloning wasn't just an experiment in science fiction—there were very real potential medical uses for cloning.

Ethics aside, Dolly's successful birth was groundbreaking scientifically. Somatic cells are differentiated adult cells, and typically they have deactivated the genes they don't need for their functions. For example, a somatic cell from the digestive system may have deactivated the genes in it that control, say, respiratory system functions. For a successful cloning to occur, all of the deactivated genes must be reactivated so that the full genetic blueprint can be used for the developing embryo. Dolly's birth proved that this could be done.

Many scientists followed up this success by experimenting with cloning by nuclear transfer in other species of mammals. Various teams of scientists successfully used somatic cell nuclear transfer to clone other mammals, some of them transgenic. One team was able to clone a male mouse, whereas all previous clones were female.

These successes also led scientists to experiment with creating animals from endangered or extinct species, similar to the idea behind the successful book and movie *Jurassic Park*—except, of course, not with dinosaurs!

Scientists used eggs from animals closely related to the endangered or extinct species and attempted to recreate the endangered or extinct animals.

In 2009, one team became the first scientists to successfully clone an extinct animal when they created an extinct Spanish mountain goat known as a bucardo. Their experiment resulted in a live birth, but the goat died shortly after birth from a lung defect.

PRIMATES: MOVING ONE STEP CLOSER to HUMANS

Technically, humans are primates. However, there are many species of primates, and humans are just one of them. In 1997, scientists Li Meng, John Ely, Richard Stouffer, and Don Wolf brought the cloning conversation a step closer to humans by attempting to clone primates through nuclear transfer of embryonic cells. They used the same process as in many previous cloning experiments. They used nuclei from embryonic cells early in the development process—this time from rhesus monkeys. They fused the cells with egg cells that had the nucleus removed and then implanted the developing embryos into surrogate mother monkeys. While they successfully cloned twenty-nine embryos, only two resulted in live births. Still, this was enough to show that primates can be cloned—and in theory, human cloning might someday be possible, given that humans are primates.

STEM CELLS: The FUTURE of MEDICINE?

Stem cells are undifferentiated, which means they can be used to create infinitely more cells that can ultimately differentiate for various functions. In recent years, they have been the subject of much interest for scientists because in theory, they could be useful in treating many diseases and conditions and for testing new drugs for safety and effectiveness. However, there are some ethical concerns with using stem cells because the most useful ones come from embryos. Stem cells can come from adults, but they are in short supply in adults and are more limited in their usability than embryonic stem cells.

It's no surprise then that some recent scientific experimentation in the field of cloning has centered on stem cells. In 2007, American biologist Shoukhrat Mitalipov and a team of scientists used a somatic cell from an adult rhesus monkey and transferred its nucleus into a monkey egg cell that had the nucleus removed. An embryo developed, and its cells grew in a lab culture. These cells were stem cells, and their successful creation suggested that perhaps somatic cells could be used from an adult human to generate stem cells that could then be used for medical purposes.

In 2013, Mitalipov and his team took the experiment to the next level and used somatic cell nuclear transfer to successfully create a human embryo that could be used for stem cells. The donor cell was from a baby with a rare genetic disorder—in other words, they created an embryo from the baby in an effort to see whether they could generate stem cells they could in theory use in research or treatment for the baby's condition. While this is a major accomplishment in the scientific world, it's easy to see how there could be ethical concerns about "creating" humans for the purposes of research or treatment.

ALL the PIECES of the PUZZLE

These scientists all contributed to the current body of scientific knowledge about cloning, genetics, and related scientific fields. Technically, this history could be traced back even further. Gregor Mendel's work in the mid-1800s formed the basis of the study of genetics, and even though its importance wasn't truly recognized until decades later, Mendel's work remains part of the foundation of genetics as we know it.

However, interest in genetics and heredity didn't start with Mendel. A Babylonian tablet from more than six thousand years ago demonstrates that citizens of that ancient time were interested in inherited characteristics in horses, for example. Ancient carvings describe experiments in the cross-pollination of date palms as well.

In Tianjin, China, Zhao Xin (*front*) and his team successfully cloned pigs with robotic technology.

Clearly, genetics has been on people's minds for thousands of years, in some form or another.

The citizens of ancient times may not have had the scientific knowledge to consider cloning, but they wondered about heredity and traits and about how to breed for certain desirable traits—a first building block to the science of cloning.

Even now, with scientists actively working on cloning, there are countless other scientists working on related fields that help inform the science of cloning and further discovery in the field. Some of these scientists focus on cells and molecules, while others research how different diseases impact the body as a whole. With communication and technology today, scientists can collaborate even when they work in different places around the world. Without these scientists and without their hypotheses and discoveries, cloning would not have advanced to where it is today. In the world of scientific discovery, scientists find the pieces of a puzzle that eventually combine to form a rich body of knowledge.

The next step, having looked at the work of these scientists, is to look at the discovery itself. How exactly does cloning work? What problems does it help us solve?

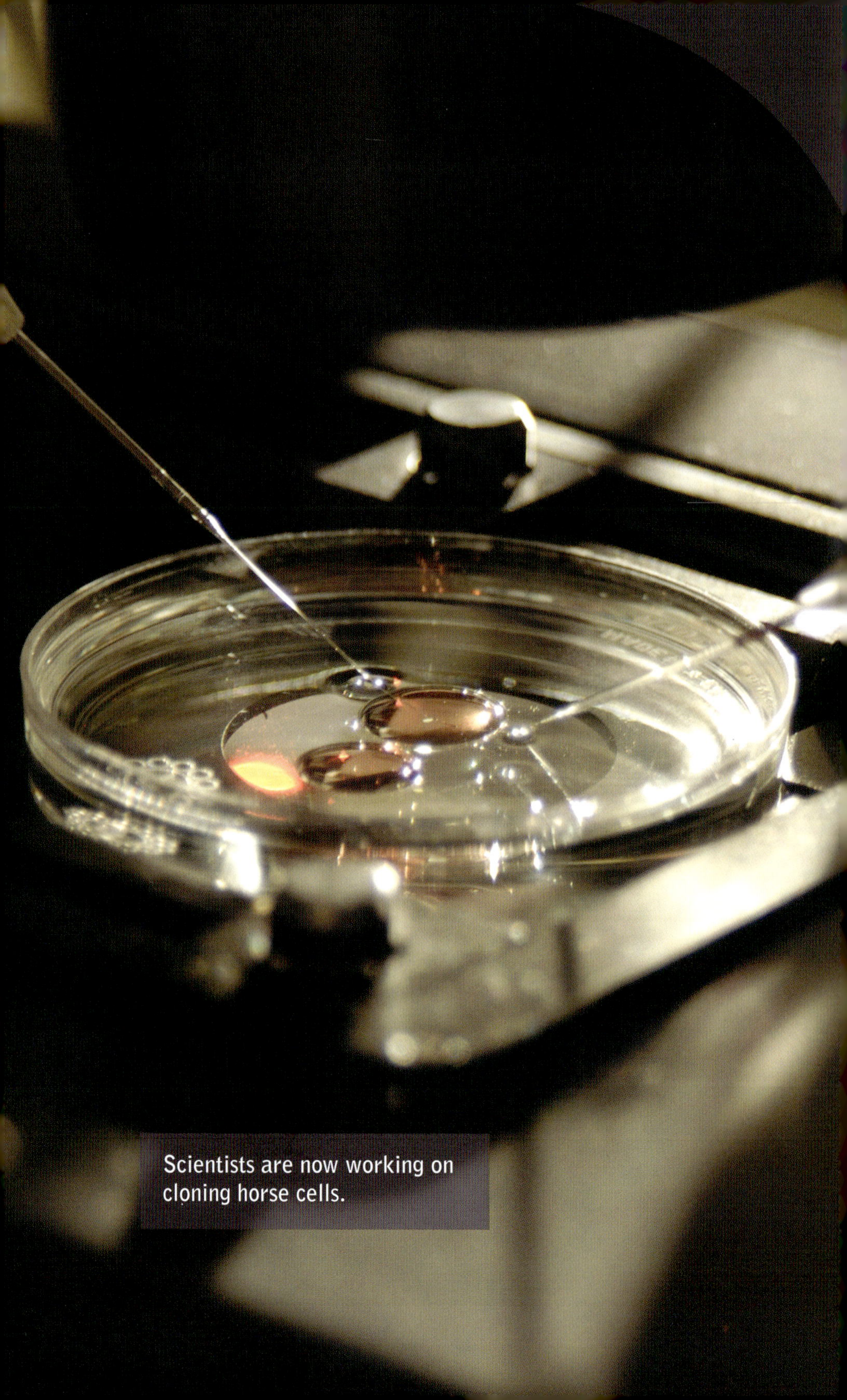

Scientists are now working on cloning horse cells.

CHAPTER 4

The Discovery of Cloning

In some ways, cloning seems like a relatively simple process. Genetic material is removed from one cell and placed into another. But, in reality, the process is incredibly complicated, even at the molecular level—that is, the smallest level at which cloning takes place. It's not surprising that cloning took years to refine and is still in the relatively early stages of development, given the level of complexity involved in the process.

MOLECULAR CLONING

The molecular level is the smallest level at which cloning is done. Molecular cloning involves creating molecules of recombinant DNA, or DNA that is formed manually by combining genetic material.

At first, this was a very difficult process because isolating and removing specific molecules of DNA could not be easily accomplished. But, in the late 1960s, scientists discovered

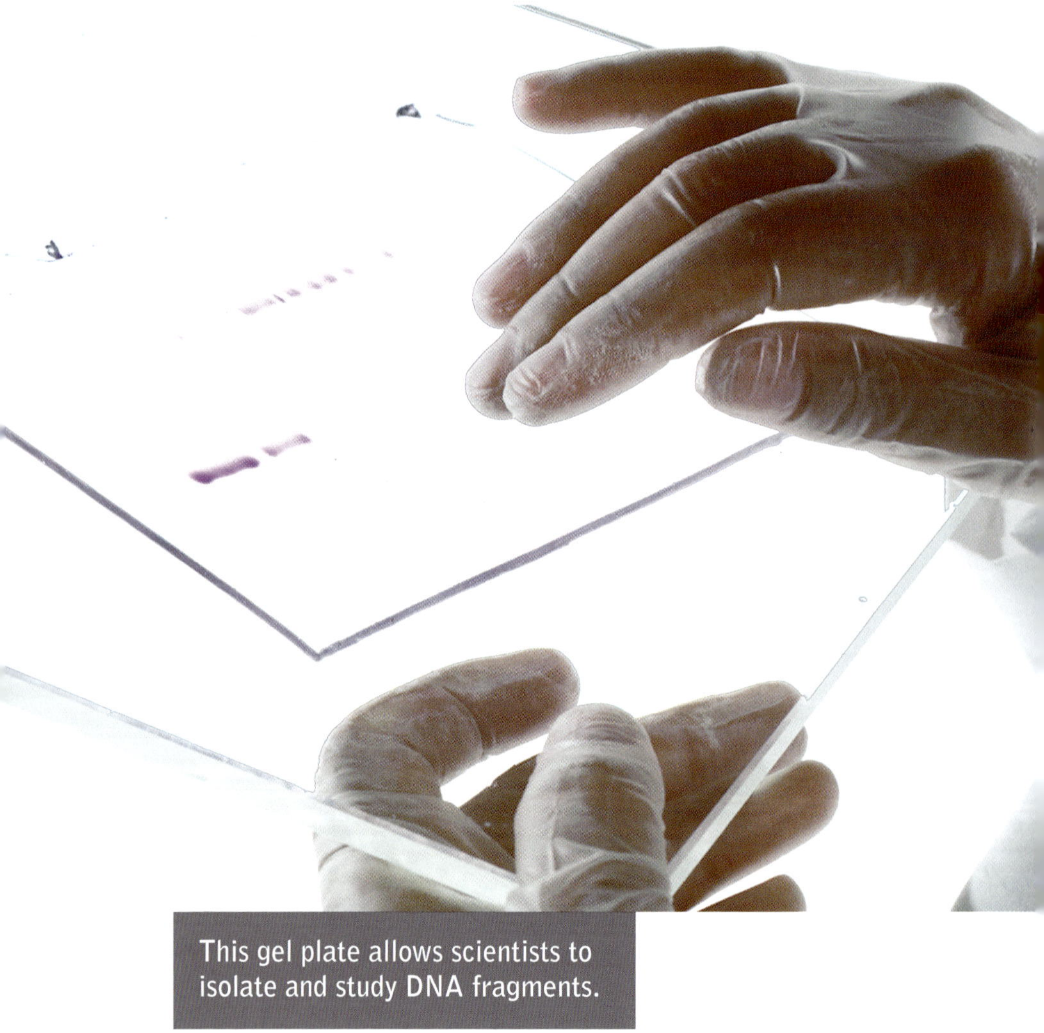

This gel plate allows scientists to isolate and study DNA fragments.

certain enzymes that can specifically and selectively cut molecules of DNA; these enzymes are known as restriction endonucleases. Suddenly, segmenting tiny molecules of DNA was much easier.

These segmented molecules could then be inserted into a vector's DNA sequence, adding the genetic material to the vector's genetic material without disrupting the vector's original DNA sequence.

In general, there are four steps to the molecular cloning process. First, targeted DNA fragments must be isolated. These fragments are sometimes called "inserts" because they will be inserted into another DNA sequence. Using restriction endonucleases, these inserts are then cut and placed into a vector for cloning, which creates recombinant DNA molecules. Often, these vectors are plasmids, which are useful for cloning in a laboratory setting. Then, these recombinant plasmids are transformed into bacteria or other hosts that can effectively reproduce. Finally, the hosts that contain the recombinant plasmids are screened and selected.

This four-step process, while seemingly simple, involves a number of factors for each step.

Cutting

At the cutting or digestion stage of the process, restriction endonucleases are a key factor. Scientists had seen these endonucleases as early as 1952, but they weren't entirely sure what their purpose or function was. They could see that the endonucleases seemed to make certain strains of bacteria more resistant to infection by bacteriophage, but they weren't exactly sure how.

In 1968, Swiss microbiologist and geneticist Werner Arber discovered that the strains of bacteria resistant to bacteriophage infection were actually degrading and cutting into pieces the bacteriophage DNA. He theorized that the bacteriophage-resistant cells must express an enzyme that not only degraded the bacteriophage DNA but also protected the cell's own DNA from that same degradation. In other words, the cell could destroy the bacteriophage while protecting itself.

Working with American microbiologist Stuart Linn, Arber isolated a modification and related restriction enzyme that worked to degrade the DNA in *E. coli* bacteria while also protecting the bacteriophage-resistant cell, proving Arber's original theory.

Arber and Linn's work was taken further by scientists Hamilton Smith, Dan Nathans, and Kathleen Danna, whose work isolated how restriction endonucleases cut specific DNA sequences and how that process could be used to map genomes. In 1978, Arber, Smith, and Nathans jointly won the Nobel Prize in Physiology or Medicine for their contributions to genome sequencing.

Restriction endonucleases also cut the DNA in the cloning vector at the place where the insert DNA will be placed.

Assembling

Just as enzymes were responsible for specifically and selectively cutting DNA fragments and for cleaving DNA in the cloning vector to prepare for the insert DNA, so were enzymes responsible for then assembling DNA fragments

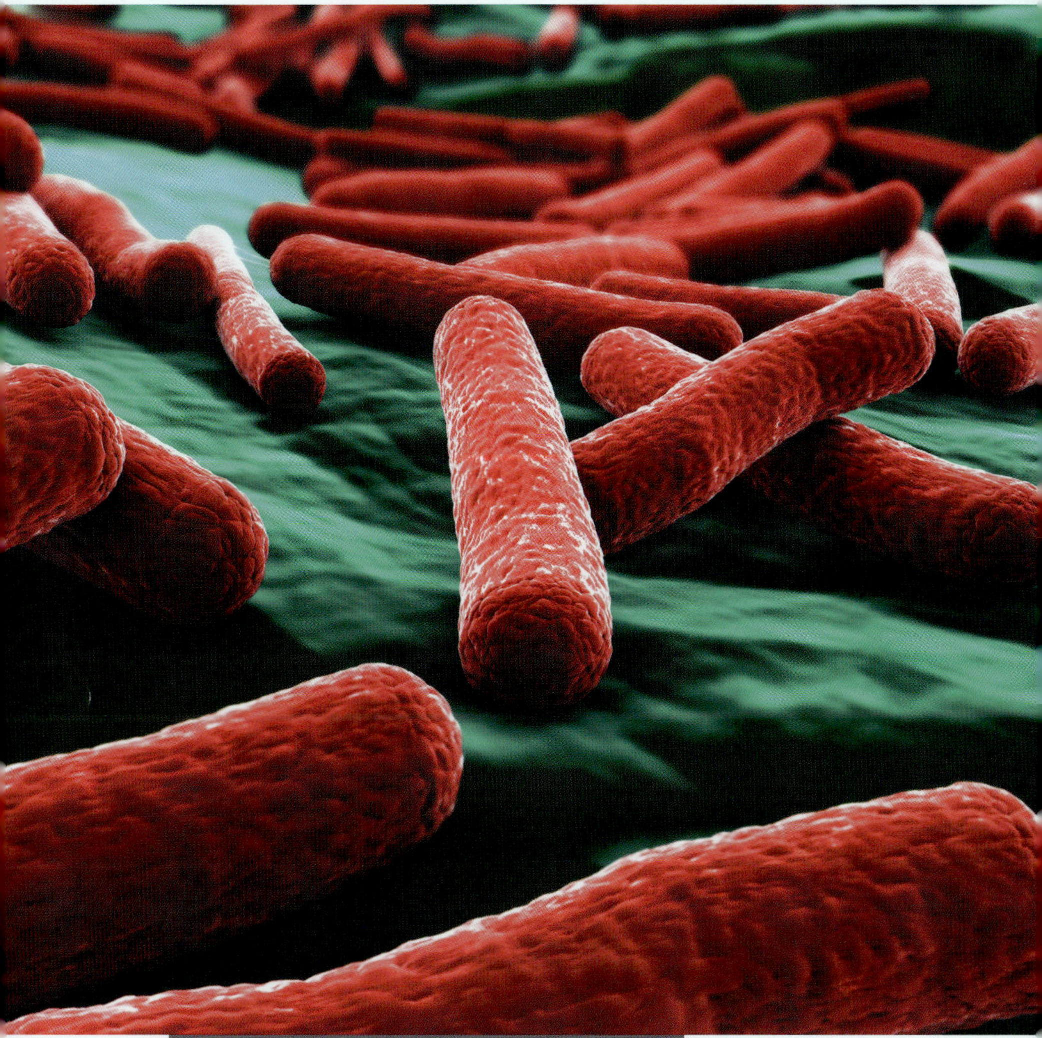

Seen up close through a microscope, *E. coli* bacteria look like deep red rods.

in the vector. This type of enzyme is called a DNA ligase. These specific ligases join strands of DNA by acting as catalysts in the formation of a specific chemical bond called a phosphodiester bond. This assembly stage is also called ligation because of the role played by DNA ligases.

DNA ligases were discovered around the same time as restriction endonucleases, and once scientists learned how they could use restriction endonucleases to cut segments of DNA, it didn't take long before they used DNA ligases to then combine those cut fragments with other segments of DNA, creating recombinant DNA. The first recombinant DNA molecule was created in 1972 by biochemist Paul Berg, who jointly won the 1980 Nobel Prize in Chemistry for his contribution to the field of biochemistry with respect to his creation of the first strand of recombinant DNA.

In the lab, extracted DNA that will be cloned is purified to remove contaminating proteins, RNA, and smaller molecules. This occurs before the insert DNA is placed into the vector.

Transforming

For molecular cloning to occur, recombinant DNA needed to be able to propagate, or spread. Often, this is done by transfer to bacteria, though other host organisms are sometimes used. The first successful transformation of a recombinant DNA molecule was achieved in 1973, when scientists Herbert Boyer, Stanley Cohen, and A. C. Chang transformed a recombinant DNA molecule into the bacteria *E. coli*.

In fact, most molecular cloning uses a laboratory strain of the bacteria *E. coli*. *E. coli* is rather notorious because some strains of it can cause fairly serious—sometimes fatal—illnesses, such as diarrhea, urinary tract infections, and pneumonia. However, many strains of *E. coli* are harmless, and the laboratory strains of *E. coli* used as host organisms are widely available and allow recombinant organisms to reproduce rapidly.

In the lab, *E. coli* is generally used with a plasmid cloning vector, which can clone and make many copies of genes and can also be used to express particular genes. However, if the DNA to be cloned is a particularly long sequence, sometimes bacterial or yeast artificial chromosome vectors are used instead. There are also specialized host-vector systems when molecular cloning is for a specialized application, but in general, cloning occurs in a bacterial plasmid and then may be sub-cloned in a more specialized vector.

Not all host organisms will accept recombinant DNA, which means there's a failure rate in this process. To try to make it as efficient as possible, sometimes scientists will purposely destroy cells that have not taken up recombinant DNA, leaving only the cells that do accept recombinant DNA. It's a sort of manually enforced survival of the fittest!

Refining the Process

By the early 1970s, molecular cloning had been achieved, but it was an inefficient process. Restriction endonucleases, being natural substances, weren't always reliable—there was no standardized purification process for them. The plasmids used for cloning in the lab weren't always readily available and could be difficult to work with. There were limitations to the amount of insert DNA that scientists could isolate at that time.

Scientists in the years that followed made many advances in the field. Scientists working with Herbert Boyer set to work isolating a small vector that could be used as a general cloning plasmid, and they identified it in 1977.

Screening vectors was an issue too. Plasmids could self-ligate without insert DNA, and those plasmids were not desired for cloning. Scientists Joachim Messing and Jeffrey Vieira created a screening tool that could isolate plasmids with DNA inserts from those without. It was essentially a blue-white system in which bacteria containing plasmids with DNA inserts would show as white in a specific culture medium, while bacteria containing plasmids without DNA inserts would show as blue. Tag genes are now typically used for this type of screening. Tag genes are inserted into the sequence so scientists can easily screen for cells containing the insert DNA.

Further, scientists worked to better prepare vectors for insertion of recombinant DNA. They learned that alkaline phosphatases could remove phosphate groups from the ends of DNA, and a particular phosphatase could prevent the vector from self-ligating, which increased the number of plasmids that were successfully ligated with the DNA insert. In other words, the vector molecules treated with alkaline phosphatase could only replicate if insert DNA was placed into the cleavage site on the vector DNA.

DNA sequencing furthered molecular cloning technology. DNA sequencing is generally what it sounds like: determining the sequence of nucleotides in a DNA molecule. This helps scientists identify specific recombinant DNA molecules in a strand of DNA, as well as identify new genes or gene mutations. Two methods of DNA sequencing were developed in the late 1970s: Maxam-Gilbert sequencing, which was groundbreaking at the time but is now no longer used much, and Sanger sequencing, which was widely used until the last few years, when high-throughput sequencing became more widely used.

In the earliest years of molecular cloning, getting enough insert DNA to place into a vector was also problematic. However, American biochemist and 1993 Nobel Prize in Chemistry winner Kary Mullis addressed this problem by determining that polymerase chain reactions could take infinitesimally small quantities of DNA and amplify and clone them for insertion into the vector.

Finally, specialized cloning techniques have been developed that have made molecular cloning more efficient. These techniques make use of the properties of unique enzymes and essentially modify the structures of the molecules so that they can be ligated more effectively into the vector.

Molecular cloning techniques are still being advanced and further developed, but in the past nearly half century, the initial discovery of molecular cloning has come a long way.

CELL CLONING

Moving one step up in the complexity of material, scientists can also clone cells. Molecules are parts of cells, so cells contain multiple different molecules.

Cells contain a multitude of genetic information, so when a cell is cloned, all of the genetic information is

Technologies for Harvesting Embryonic Stem Cells

Embryonic stem cells used to be harvested by a process called somatic cell nuclear transfer (SCNT). This is the same process used in many early cloning experiments. The nucleus is removed from any non–sex cell (called a somatic cell) and is implanted into a donor egg whose nucleus has been removed, called an enucleated egg. The donor egg, believing it has been fertilized, begins the normal process of dividing and forming an embryo. Then, the richest cells from the inner cell mass in the blastocyst are removed, which destroys the embryo.

However, a new method called altered nuclear transfer (ANT) offers a solution to the ethical issues surrounding destroying an embryo. In ANT, scientists reprogram the nucleus of the somatic cell before they transfer it into the enucleated egg. The resulting egg produces stem cells, but it does not become an embryo. In other words, there is no potential for life in it.

The stem cells are removed from the resulting egg earlier than in the process of SCNT. Traditionally, scientists using the SCNT process have removed stem cells when the embryo is a mass of approximately one hundred cells. Scientists using the ANT method instead extract a stem cell when the fertilized egg is only two days old, consisting of an eight-cell embryo called a morula. The extracted cell is called a blastomere.

Technically, even a true eight-cell embryo (meant for development of human life) can survive with only seven blastomeres. When couples undergo fertility treatment, doctors and scientists often remove one blastomere at the eight-cell stage to check for genetic conditions. (If a genetic condition is found, then the developing embryo is generally not used for reproduction.) Once embryos have been determined to have no genetic abnormality, fertility doctors can implant them into the mother with only seven blastomeres, and the embryo will, if all goes right, continue to develop into a baby.

So, it is promising that a single embryonic stem cell can be extracted without harming a developing embryo, but it isn't the most efficient process. With the older SCNT process of harvesting stem cells, scientists would typically get many from a single embryo.

Stem cells can be stored for a long time in liquid nitrogen.

identical. (If the cloned cell has a genetic mutation, however, it would no longer be referred to as a clone because the genetic information wouldn't be identical anymore.)

Cell cloning can happen naturally, such as when single-celled organisms like bacteria reproduce asexually. Some plants also have the ability to reproduce asexually. Cell cloning also technically happens naturally in the case of identical twins, when one fertilized egg splits into two embryos that have nearly identical genetic information. Identical twins aren't called clones because as the embryo develops, some subtle differences always occur, but at that very first stage, when the fertilized egg splits into two, it's technically a natural cloning process.

Artificial cell cloning, performed by scientists, is also sometimes called therapeutic cloning because it's generally done to create cells to repair or replace diseased or injured tissues in the body. These cells are often embryonic stem cells, but technically any kind of cell can be cloned. Stem cells are most often cloned because they have the ability to be differentiated so they are effective in repairing or replacing specific tissue types. In other words, they're quite versatile and thus very useful.

The richest, most useful stem cells are embryonic stem cells harvested from an embryo that is only a few days old, when it is a ball of approximately one hundred cells and is known as a blastocyst. Stem cells can also be gathered from bone marrow and umbilical cord blood, but those stem cells can't differentiate into as many different kinds of cells as embryonic stem cells can.

Embryonic stem cells have been collected from fertilized eggs left over from fertility treatments. The couples involved have donated the fertilized eggs for research purposes, so legally there is no issue. Researchers aren't taking fertilized eggs without obtaining consent from the parents. But ethically, some consider it another issue.

Human embryonic stem cell research and harvesting runs into issues of ethics because harvesting stem cells from an embryo at that stage can destroy the embryo. To many pro-life people, that is akin to murder because the embryo has the potential for life and it is destroyed. However, there have been advancements made in science that may allow researchers to harvest stem cells without destroying the embryo.

While stem cells get most of the attention as far as cell cloning is concerned, there is another method of cell cloning that is used in fertility treatments. It's a bit simpler than stem-cell cloning. It essentially imitates the way that identical twins form.

Identical twins form when a single fertilized egg splits into two, and each resulting cell begins dividing and replicating. In the process called artificial embryo twinning, scientists essentially force this to happen multiple times. They place an embryo in the earliest stages in a Petri dish and separate each cell from the embryo into individual cells. Those individual cells are all genetically identical because they all developed from the same fertilized egg. When those individual cells are separated and allowed to develop, each one begins dividing and replicating, essentially forming multiple "twin" embryos that can then be implanted into a mother, where the hope is that at least one or more will develop into a fetus and then into a baby.

Scientists in China successfully cloned macaques (a species of primate) in 2018.

This is partly why there is a high incidence of twins or other multiple births in couples undergoing fertility treatments. Doctors often implant multiple embryos in the hope that at least one will continue to develop into a baby. Sometimes, more than one develops, and the mother ultimately gives birth to two or more babies. (There are other factors involved in fertility treatment that can also contribute to multiple births, but the creation and implantation of multiple embryos is one.)

ORGANISM CLONING

At the most complex level of cloning is organism cloning, which is also sometimes called reproductive cloning. The end goal of this process is to create a whole other genetically identical organism. This type of cloning is what resulted in Dolly the sheep, and it is how other animals and even domestic pets have been cloned.

Molecular and cell cloning can both be done in a laboratory, but organism cloning is more complex, and thus, it cannot be entirely done in a lab culture. Animal cells usually have to grow inside a host (or "mother"), so they cannot be cloned exclusively in a lab culture, like plant cells, stem cells, and molecules can.

The process used for organism cloning is called nuclear transplantation. This means that the nucleus of a donor cell is removed and placed in an enucleated host cell. Often the process used is SCNT, just as in cell cloning. This process is relatively old by science standards, having first been performed in the 1950s, but it is still used today in many cases.

Technically, there are two methods of achieving nuclear transplantation. In the first method, scientists remove the nucleus of a somatic cell using a needle and inject it into an enucleated egg. The second method uses electrical current to fuse the whole somatic cell with an enucleated egg. Either way, the egg with the transplanted nucleus begins to develop into an embryo. Either way, the cloned animal technically has three mothers—the one that produced the somatic cell from which the nucleus was extracted, the one that produced the empty cell that the nucleus was transferred to, and the host mother that carries the embryo to term.

In Washington, DC, protestors express their views against human cloning.

In early experiments, it was thought that the donor nucleus had to come from an early-stage embryo in order for cloning to be successful. However, that was later disproven. In 1958, British developmental biologist John Gurdon appeared to successfully produce cloned frogs from cells later in the development process than the earliest experiments had tested. There was some debate over whether Gurdon's findings were accurate, though, because some thought Gurdon might have used stem cells in his experiment, rather than differentiated adult cells. But in 2002, molecular biologist Konrad Hochedlinger and biologist Rudolf Jaenisch proved that mouse clones could be created from mature white blood cells (which are already differentiated), essentially proving Gurdon's theory.

When nuclear transplantation is used for organism cloning, the developing embryo must be transferred into a host to continue development and result in a live birth. It can only survive for a limited time in a lab culture. This process has no guarantees, though. Just like in regular reproduction for organisms, sometimes it's successful and sometimes it isn't. Sometimes the host organism does not successfully carry the implanted embryo to term. Sometimes the embryos develop abnormally for reasons having nothing to do with the host—just as naturally created embryos sometimes develop abnormally.

The sheep Dolly, notable for being the first mammal successfully cloned from an adult somatic cell, is a perfect example. Scientists at the Roslin Institute in Scotland made 277 attempts to successfully clone a sheep. From those attempts, only twenty-nine embryos survived longer than six days. Finally, one survived—Dolly.

Since Dolly, other animals have been successfully cloned, but the greater scientific interest lay in what the successful cloning of Dolly and the animals that followed meant for stem-cell research. The successful birth of Dolly showed scientists that differentiated adult cells (in Dolly's case, mammary cells from an adult sheep) could be used to create an embryo with stem cells that are a genetic match for the organism that donated the adult cell. In other words, a cell could, in theory, be taken from a human suffering from a disease or condition, and the nucleus could be transferred into an enucleated cell that would then result in an embryo growing stem cells. Those stem cells could then be used to grow tissue to help treat or replace the diseased tissue.

Later scientific research showed that personalized stem cells can also be created by reprogramming adult cells into stem cells, meaning that no embryo needs to be created and destroyed to obtain the stem cells. Obviously, this removes some of the ethical concerns surrounding cloning human cells.

All of this development was possible because of the manner in which Dolly was successfully cloned. So, while cloning mammals may not have had the desired outcome—the ability to easily create cloned mammals—it still contributed positively to the body of knowledge in the cloning field.

In 2007, Ian Wilmut, the embryologist who led the team that produced Dolly, announced that he did not think SCNT, which was used to create Dolly, would ever be a viable method for cloning humans. It was too inefficient and had too many ethical implications with the high rate of failures. Instead, Wilmut felt the later method for reprogramming

The bacteria shown here are used in the process of gene reproduction and cloning.

adult cells into stem cells without the need to create an embryo was much more promising, without the ethical issues surrounding the method in which Dolly was created.

In the years since scientists first successfully cloned Dolly, other mammals have been cloned, including cows, cats, dogs, deer, horses, mules, oxen, rabbits, rats, and even a rhesus monkey. The monkey is as close to a human clone as science has gotten so far.

There have been a few reports from South Korea and from a fringe religious group that human embryos have been cloned successfully (the religious group even claims that their embryo grew into the first fully developed human female clone and that they have cloned twelve other humans as well), but none of those claims have proven to be true.

A large part of why humans have not yet been cloned successfully is the ethical concerns surrounding cloning. However, on a strictly scientific level, there is another reason why human cloning would be very difficult.

Two spindle proteins that are required for successful cell division are located close to the chromosomes in primate eggs (and humans are classified as primates). Removing a primate cell's nucleus for cloning results in the spindle proteins also being removed, which causes problems with the cell-division process necessary for cloning to occur. Also, ultraviolet light and dyes used when removing an egg's nucleus have been shown to damage primate cells.

So, in a way, we don't quite have the technology to carry out human cloning—even if we had an answer to all of the ethical concerns. For the time being, human cloning will remain the stuff of science-fiction movies and books. The exception, of course, is human stem cells, which hold great potential. Given the benefits of stem cells as a way to study disease and generate tissue to treat devastating diseases and conditions, it's very likely that research into stem-cell cloning will continue.

Protestors in London took part in a demonstration against using cloned animals as a food source.

CHAPTER 5

Cloning Today

Cloning is not only relevant today. In many ways, it's at the forefront of research. Stem-cell research is a hot-button topic due to the ethical concerns surrounding it and the promise it holds for scientists potentially developing treatments and cures for conditions that so far have eluded them.

The implications of molecular cloning and animal cloning for drug production and medical research are also increasingly relevant today, as humans are living longer and, in some cases, facing health concerns that people in past generations may not have faced.

The building blocks that led to cloning unfolded over more than a century, but now that cloning is at the forefront of medical science and research, its impact cannot be overstated. Let's begin by exploring some of the ethical debates surrounding the science of cloning.

The GREAT ETHICAL DEBATE

Much debate on ethical implications has swirled around the discovery and implication of cloning technology. The debates are often affected by people's beliefs, but they also depend on the type of cloning being considered.

Ethics of Molecular Cloning

Molecular cloning involves genetic engineering. Scientists create recombinant DNA designed to address an issue, and then they clone it for therapeutic or commercial use. One debate behind this is whether it is ethical to modify an existing genome.

People with strong religious beliefs sometimes take issue with this type of cloning because they believe humans and animals were created by a supreme being and that supreme being's creation should not be tampered with. They believe scientists are playing the role of God when they alter the genome.

However, the opposing argument is that the purpose of molecular cloning is often to help people. Scientists create recombinant DNA in an effort to treat diseases and conditions and to make organisms more resilient. Some argue that a supreme being would have no problem with that, since the intention is to help people. Others argue that whether or not a supreme being exists is irrelevant. This is simply scientific research in the name of positive progress.

Another argument is that altering DNA is a slippery slope. While few people would argue that creating recombinant DNA in the name of combatting a devastating disease like cancer is a bad thing, it leads to another question: If we can alter DNA to fight disease, then could we potentially alter it to eradicate certain genetic conditions?

This a hot-button topic in certain disability communities. Down syndrome is a genetic condition. In fact, it is the most commonly occurring genetic condition, even though it is still fairly rare. It occurs when the fertilized egg has an extra copy of the twenty-first chromosome. As the fertilized cell replicates, every single cell in the embryo and resulting human being has an extra twenty-first chromosome.

This extra chromosome causes global developmental delays. People with Down syndrome are intellectually and developmentally disabled. While they can go on to live long, healthy, fulfilling lives, some people believe that it would be better to remove this genetic variation from the human population. No one asks to be disabled, they argue. If there's a way to stop it from happening, why wouldn't we?

The opposite side argues that the human population is made up of genetic variations, of which Down syndrome is just one. If society starts cherry-picking which genetic variations are desirable and which aren't, they argue, we are starting down a very slippery slope that could end up looking like Adolf Hitler's vision for Germany. Hitler was determined to create a master race that did not include Jews, disabled people, homosexuals, and many other groups he deemed to be less than perfect. Those against using cloning technology to potentially end conditions like Down syndrome point to the similarities and ask whether that's a road we really should go down.

Some people wonder if cloning could lead to a form of eugenics in which conditions such as Down syndrome are eradicated.

Molecular cloning can also be used to develop plants with desirable characteristics, and this touches the controversial topic of genetically modified organisms, or GMOs. In the eyes of many Americans, GMOs have a well-deserved bad reputation. Scientists alter the genetic material in certain crops, such as wheat and corn, to create hardier, more drought-resistant crops, crops that produce higher yields, and more.

Critics of GMOs ask what this does to people's bodies when these products are ingested. For example, some suggest that the increasing rates of gluten intolerance in the population may be due to people's bodies being unable to effectively digest genetically modified wheat. Some have speculated that perhaps the skyrocketing numbers of autism diagnoses in the United States might be linked to Americans' consumption of GMO products.

The truth is, the answers to questions about GMOs often can't be answered yet. GMOs are a relatively new technology in the grand scheme of agricultural science in the United States, and the long-term effects of genetically modifying crops are unknown. Scientists have done numerous studies on the safety of GMO crops and report that they are safe for consumption, but there are many variables involved. The truth is that their safety or danger can't be proved for certain either way yet.

However, the opposing argument is that GMO crops have led to much lower death rates in developing countries that rely on crops to feed their populations. In some countries, in years where crop yields were low because of drought or other environmental causes, people

GMO crops, such as corn, are banned in some countries and are eyed with great suspicion by many Americans.

regularly died of starvation or malnutrition. They argue that by developing crops that can withstand drought and other harsh conditions, scientists are saving lives. By developing crops with higher yields, they are feeding more people and helping to combat malnutrition globally.

Ethics of Cell Cloning

Cell cloning most commonly refers to stem-cell cloning, a topic that is fraught with debate. Stem cells can be obtained from adults, but they are typically not as versatile or as plentiful as the stem cells that can be obtained from developing embryos.

When embryonic stem-cell research began, the ethical nature of it became a major concern because harvesting stem cells from embryos meant destroying the embryos. For many people with pro-life views, destroying an embryo is the same as aborting a fetus or killing a human. They view an embryo as a life and argue that a life should never be destroyed.

Even among people who are politically pro-choice, there can be similar ethical concerns. There are a fair number of people who believe that a woman should have the right to choose to have an abortion but who also

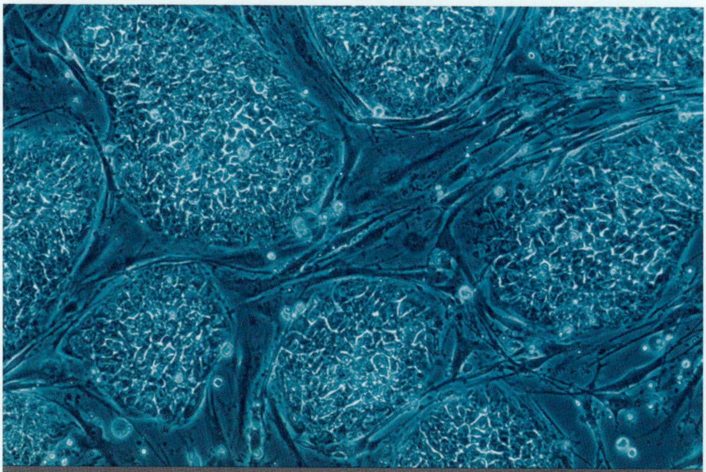

Embryonic stem cells such as these can potentially be used to restore damaged tissues.

believe that destroying an embryo in the name of science is ethically concerning.

The other side of the argument often says that the embryos from which stem cells are harvested were never going to become a person anyway. Those embryos often consist of the unused ones from fertility clinics, and the parents of the embryos have signed away their rights to the embryos and donated them to scientific research. Thus, people in favor of embryonic stem-cell research argue that there is nothing ethically wrong about using the embryos for science. And, they argue, the goal is using the cells for therapeutic efforts. Scientists use the stem cells to develop new treatments (and hopefully cures) for serious diseases and conditions.

Some also argue the point of when a life begins. There is no hard line as to when an embryo or a fetus is officially a life. Some believe life begins at the moment of conception—a fertilized egg is a life, even before it has begun to divide and replicate. Others believe life begins even before that. Stopping a sperm cell from fertilizing an egg is technically ending a potential life. Others set arbitrary times during gestation when they believe life begins. Generally, a human pregnancy is considered viable when a fetus has a chance of survival outside of the womb, so some consider life beginning around the time a fetus is viable (usually somewhere around the twenty-third week of pregnancy). Others consider life as beginning when a woman enters the second trimester of pregnancy, around the thirteenth week of a pregnancy. Some consider life as beginning when a baby is born.

This determination of when life begins is at the heart of some ethical debates over embryonic stem-cell research. If an embryo is considered a life, then many believe it should not be destroyed.

In recent years, this debate has become a bit less heated because scientists are developing new methods of harvesting embryonic stem cells that don't necessarily involve destroying the embryo. There is still some debate because some believe that the harvested stem cells could technically grow into human beings if allowed, but the debate is far less when scientists are not actively destroying embryos to obtain the stem cells.

Ethics of Organism Cloning

When scientists discovered how to clone molecules, cells, and, particularly, animals, the public immediately began to wonder whether that would someday lead to human cloning, and an ethical debate flared.

One argument was that human cloning would reduce the diversity in humankind. Most people believe that there is strength in diversity—not only in the fact that it creates a richer, more interesting and varied society of people, but also because when a species is too genetically similar, it can lead to health concerns. (This is why inbreeding is not recommended in human or animal populations. It's generally not an issue in humans because of social taboos against it, but inbreeding does occur in dogs, when dog breeders try to breed dogs that share similarly desirable traits. The result can be dogs with significant health issues.)

Longlong: The First Cloned Gene-Edited Dog

Many people are in favor of cloning for its benefits to medical research. But, for some, it can be hard to support cloning when looking into the warm eyes of a puppy. Lab animals have long been used for research; often they are rodents such as mice or rats, and sometimes they are other mammals, such as monkeys. But few expect to see house pets as experimental subjects.

In China, scientists have taken a step to clone the first gene-edited dog, a beagle named Longlong.

According to the technical director at Sinogene, the Chinese biotech company that cloned the puppy from a gene-edited dog named Apple, "Dogs share the most inheritable disease with human beings, which makes them the best disease models to study." So, when scientists wanted to better study atherosclerosis, they decided to modify Apple's genome to make the dog develop the disease. Then they cloned Apple three times, creating Longlong and two other puppies, Xixi and Nuonuo. All four dogs are genetically identical, and all of the dogs will develop atherosclerosis.

People for the Ethical Treatment of Animals (PETA) described Sinogene's action as "unethical" and "inherently cruel." Sinogene disagrees, though. It asserts that it needs the dogs in order to be able to continue research into atherosclerosis, which affects more than 15.8 million Americans and can cause heart disease, heart attacks, and strokes, among other conditions. Before it was able to clone the gene-edited dogs, Sinogene had to force-feed the canine subjects with sugary, fatty meals so that the dogs would develop atherosclerosis. Sinogene claims the cloning method of getting research subjects is more humane. Eugene Redmond, the director of Neural Transplantation and Repair at Yale University's School of Medicine, agrees. Redmond stated, "[M]aking better animal models more focused on the problem of interest could lead to better therapy development, [and] safer treatments, with fewer animals required."

Research into atherosclerosis could potentially lead to millions of lives saved but at the cost of cloning animals destined to die of a devastating illness. Whether the benefits outweigh the drawbacks is the eternal question.

Dolly the sheep is pictured here with one of her creators, Dr. Ian Wilmut.

Another argument against human cloning is the same as the argument against molecular cloning: Could it lead to a society where people with less desirable genetic variations are eventually removed from the human gene pool? Would it lead to eugenics, like Hitler's Nazi Germany or various genocides throughout history?

However, many arguments for human cloning involve therapeutic benefits for humans. For example, some suggest that organism cloning could allow scientists to create genetically identical donors for people needing transplants, such as leukemia patients who need bone marrow transplants. Rejection of organs or bone marrow is a common difficulty in transplants coming from other people, and creating genetically identical donors would, in theory, remove the risk of rejection.

Cloning for the purpose of harvesting organs comes with its own set of concerns. Some people worry that if the technology is developed to clone organs efficiently, it could lead to people being created solely for the purpose of harvesting organs. This idea was explored by the Nobel Prize–winning British author Kazuo Ishiguro in his novel *Never Let Me Go*, which was made into a popular film. The story probes the lives of three students who must come to terms with the fact that they were cloned in order to donate their vital organs.

Others suggest that couples whose sperm or eggs are unable to be used to conceive a child naturally or with intervention could have a child with genetic information from the parents if human cloning were developed.

Another argument against cloning surrounds the safety of the process. Organism cloning doesn't have a 100 percent success rate. In fact, for some mammals, the success rate is actually quite low. It took 277 tries to clone Dolly, for example! Primates are particularly difficult to clone. So, some people argue that organism cloning isn't humane because there is still a very high failure rate.

As in many arguments on a wide variety of topics, there are valid points on both sides of these ethical debates surrounding molecular, cell, and organism cloning, and it's difficult to determine a black-and-white answer. Because of that, it's likely the debate will continue for the foreseeable future.

The FUTURE of CLONING

The science of cloning has advanced relatively quickly over the past decades. But what does the future look like? There are certainly more advances to be made, techniques to be perfected, and ethical hurdles to jump.

The cloning of Dolly, now more than two decades ago, was revolutionary because it proved that a mammal could be cloned from adult somatic cells. But, it opened the door to a flood of questions about ethics and what the future landscape of cloning would look like. Indeed, Dr. Wilmut himself learned many lessons about the ethical issues at stake after he cloned Dolly:

> You would think that there are merely positive benefits to come from something new like this, but you also see that there are problems as well. So there

> is a sort of gray area in the middle, where things are not just as rosy and as satisfactory as you might like.

After Dolly, Dr. Wilmut shifted the focus of his research from somatic cell nuclear transfer to another technique—one that uses induced pluripotent stem (iPS) cells. Induced pluripotent stem cells are adult cells derived from skin or blood cells that can be reprogrammed into an embryonic-like pluripotent state. These cells hold much therapeutic potential for humans.

So, as it turns out, the future landscape doesn't look like anything out of a frightening science-fiction tale in which people are being cloned for organ harvest. Instead, researchers in organism cloning are interested in cloning as it relates to changing animals genetically for purposes such as breeding dairy cattle with no horns (so that they don't have to be dehorned, which is a painful procedure). They're also working to create a type of pig that cannot be infected by the PRRS virus, which costs the pig industry in the United States millions of dollars per year. Similarly, cloning has also been used to create cattle that are immune to mad cow disease, which is devastating to cows and fatal to humans that contract it.

Another possible future use for organism cloning is battling world hunger. Scientists have considered whether cloning animals for meat could help feed starving people in the world's developing nations. At this point, cloning is far too expensive and not efficient enough for it to be a viable solution to feeding the hungry, but it could be in the future.

Scientists in medical research also hope that therapeutic cloning may be the key to curing degenerative diseases, such as Alzheimer's and Parkinson's disease, that currently have treatments but no known cures. When ethical hurdles are cleared, many in medical research hope that processes to grow new organs from stem cells will continue to develop and that eventually it will be a viable medical treatment for many diseases and conditions.

For those who want to stray closer to the realm of science fiction, some people envision cloning as being the answer to immortality. The general idea is that a person's body could be cloned and his or her brain could be transplanted into the new body when the person's original body begins to fail as a result of aging.

This idea is a bit far-fetched at the moment, since a human brain transplant has never been done. However, in 1970, an American neurosurgeon successfully transplanted a monkey head onto another monkey's body. Post-transplant the monkey was paralyzed (because the surgery required the neurosurgeon to sever the monkey's spinal cord), but the monkey could reportedly follow objects with its eyes, eat, taste, smell, and hear.

The monkey lived only nine days, and some found the experiment to be unspeakably cruel. Still, it was a step forward in terms of research. The neurosurgeon who performed the surgery, Robert Joseph White, suggested in the 1990s that if the surgery were performed on someone like paralyzed genius physicist Stephen Hawking or paralyzed actor Christopher Reeve (both have since died), it could be revolutionary.

While this may all sound a bit odd, a startup business called Humai reportedly has immortality as a goal. Its goal is to develop the technology to freeze people's brains, create new artificial bodies, unfreeze the brains and repair any damage to them, and then place them into new artificial bodies. Critics of the company say the plan could never work, and some even wonder if the company is legitimate or simply trying to gain attention. Still, Humai is not the only organization to speculate about the possibilities cloning might have for slowing the aging process or even entertaining the idea of immortality.

The idea that cloning could lead to immortality raises significant philosophical and moral questions. It's difficult to even imagine what life would be like if this were possible. These perplexing questions have intrigued writers throughout the years.

The subject of immortality has been explored by authors from Mary Shelley to Jorge Luis Borges. Shelley's protagonist in her short story "The Mortal Immortal" suffers a life of witnessing his loved ones die around him. Borges's short story "The Immortal" examines the question of whether death itself is what gives humans the desire to pursue a significant purpose in their life. In the story, an entire society loses their will and motivation to act after achieving immortality. The novel *Tuck Everlasting* also reveals the more devastating side of immortality.

What the future holds is anyone's guess. Still, if discoveries in cloning technology continue to unfold as rapidly as they have been, there is certainly reason to believe there will be continuing development in this exciting field.

Chronology

1822 Gregor Mendel, considered by many to be the father of genetics, is born.

1856–1863
Mendel carries out his experiments on pea plants, leading him to develop several laws of modern genetics, which he publishes in 1866.

1869 Johann Friedrick Miescher extracts what is later determined to be DNA from the nuclei of white blood cells.

1885 Sea urchins are used to demonstrate the first instance of artificial embryo twinning.

1902 Hans Spemann uses salamanders to demonstrate the first artificial embryo twinning in a vertebrate.

1903 The word "clon" is used by the United States Department of Agriculture to describe a group of cells or organisms created asexually from a single ancestor.

1928 Using a fertilized salamander egg, Hans Spemann shows that embryonic development is controlled by the cell nucleus.

1944 Oswald Avery determines that the nucleic acids of cells carry genetic information.

1952 The first successful nuclear transfer is done in a frog by Robert Briggs and Thomas King. This is groundbreaking because nuclear transfer is still done today.

1953 James Watson and Francis Crick discover the structure of DNA.

1958 The first nuclear transfer is done from a differentiated cell, rather than an embryonic cell.

1969 The first gene is successfully isolated.

1970 The first restriction enzyme is successfully isolated.

1972 Paul Berg creates recombinant DNA molecules.

1975 Nuclear transfer is used to create a mammal embryo, using rabbit cells.

1977 Fred Sanger determines how to sequence DNA, which allows researchers to perform genome mapping on various species.

1984 The first mammal, a sheep, is created by nuclear transfer.

1987 The first cows are cloned using nuclear transfer from an embryonic cell.

1990 The Human Genome Project begins.

1996 The first sheep is cloned using nuclear transfer from laboratory-cultivated cells. Dolly, the first mammal cloned by somatic cell nuclear transfer, is born.

1997 The first primate (a rhesus monkey) is created using nuclear transfer from embryonic cells. The first transgenic sheep is created using nuclear transfer from genetically engineered, lab-cultivated cells. President Bill Clinton issues a five-year moratorium on using federal funds for research into human cloning.

1998–1999

Various mice, cows, and goats are cloned using somatic cell nuclear transfer, including transgenic animals, clones from fetal cells and adult cells. The first male clone is created—a mouse.

2000 The first pigs are cloned, which brings hope that pigs might someday be used for human organ transplants.

2001 A guar, an endangered species of ox, is successfully cloned but dies within forty-eight hours. A mouflon, an endangered species of wild sheep, is also successfully cloned.

2003 The sheep Dolly dies.

2004 The first commercially produced clone of a pet is created—a domestic cat.

2005 The first dog is successfully cloned in South Korea.

2007 Scientists successfully create embryonic stem cells in a rhesus monkey using somatic cell nuclear transfer.

2009 The first extinct animal is cloned—a mountain goat species known as a bucardo. The only kid to survive died minutes after it was born.

2013 Scientists create the first human embryonic stem cells from somatic cell nuclear transfer using a differentiated skin cell.

Glossary

amino acid A simple organic compound that helps make up proteins.

asexual reproduction A form of reproduction that does not involve the fusion of gametes.

atherosclerosis A disease in which fatty plaque builds up on arteries and can cause heart disease or strokes.

bacteriophage A virus that infects a bacterium and reproduces inside of it.

catalyst A substance that speeds up a chemical reaction.

centriole One of a pair of cylindrical organelles near the nucleus of an animal cell.

centromere The part of chromosomes that spindles attach to during cell division.

chromatid A threadlike strand that a chromosome divides into during cell division. Each chromosome divides into two chromatids.

chromatin A material made of protein, RNA, and DNA that makes up the chromosomes of non-bacteria organisms.

cytology The study of the structure and function of plant and animal cells.

cytoplasm The material inside a living cell, not including the nucleus.

embryology The study of embryos and their development.

epigenetic Related to nongenetic influences on gene expression.

eugenics The act of improving a human population by selectively breeding so that only desirable traits are present in the members of the population.

gametes Male and female sex cells.

genetically modified organism (GMO) Plant or animal whose genetic structure is manually altered, usually to achieve a specific outcome.

genome The complete set of genetic material in a cell or organism.

horticulturist An expert in garden cultivation and management.

hypothesis A proposed explanation made based on limited evidence, which then acts as the basis for further investigation.

in vitro fertilization A procedure in which an egg is fertilized outside the body and then implanted into the mother.

microdeletion A very small deletion of part of a gene on a chromosome.

mitosis A type of cell division in which two daughter cells are identical to the parent cell from which they divided.

nucleic acid An organic substance in all living cells with molecules consisting of a long, linked chain of nucleotides.

nucleotide The basic structural unit of nucleic acids such as DNA and RNA.

nucleus The part of a cell that contains the genetic information.

plasma membrane A very thin membrane that forms the boundary around the cytoplasm of a cell or around a vacuole in the cell.

plasmid A genetic structure in a cell that can replicate without chromosomes.

polymerase chain reaction A technique used to amplify small segments of DNA.

protist A single-celled organism, such as a protozoan, alga, or fungus.

recombinant DNA Artificially formed DNA that combines constituents from different organisms.

somatic cell All cells other than the reproductive cells of living organisms.

stem cell An undifferentiated cell that can give rise to more cells of the same type, which can then be differentiated.

transgenic Relating to an organism that contains recombinant DNA.

Further Information

BOOKS

Grant, John. *Eureka! 50 Incredible Stories of Scientific Discovery.* San Francisco, CA: Zest Books, 2016.

Jones, Phill. *Stem Cell Research and Other Cell-Related Controversies.* New York: Chelsea House Publishing, 2011.

Langwith, Jacqueline. *Cloning.* Farmington Hills, MI: Greenhaven Press, 2012.

Szumski, Bonnie. *Careers in Biotechnology.* San Diego, CA: Referencepoint Press, 2014.

Watson, James. *The Double Helix: A Personal Account of the Discovery of the Structure of DNA.* New York: Touchstone, 2001.

WEBSITES

BioInteractive

http://www.hhmi.org/biointeractive

This interactive website is full of free scientific information and resources.

HowStuffWorks

https://science.howstuffworks.com

This website features illustrations, charts, and graphics that explain in detail countless scientific topics.

Learn.Genetics

http://learn.genetics.utah.edu

Established by the University of Utah, this website provides excellent information on numerous topics related to genetics, cell biology, neuroscience, and much more.

NOVA

http://www.pbs.org/wgbh/nova

The NOVA website is full of detailed videos about scientific discoveries and topics.

Bibliography

Begley, Sharon. "Here's Why We're Still Not Cloning Humans, 20 Years After Dolly the Sheep." *Business Insider*, July 5, 2016. http://www.businessinsider.com/can-you-clone-a-human-2016-7.

Blackford, Russell. "Dolly the Sheep and the Human Cloning Debate—Twenty Years Later." *The Conversation*, August 9, 2016. http://theconversation.com/dolly-the-sheep-and-the-human-cloning-debate-twenty-years-later-63712.

Chial, Heidi. "Restriction Enzymes." Scitable, accessed February 7, 2018. https://www.nature.com/scitable/spotlight/restriction-enzymes-18458113.

"Cloning Fact Sheet." National Human Genome Research Institute, March 21, 2017. https://www.genome.gov/25020028/cloning-fact-sheet.

"Cloning Genes—Importance for Medicine and Industry." Genetics in Medicine, accessed February 7, 2018. http://medicine.jrank.org/pages/2052/Cloning-Genes-Importance-Medicine-Industry.html.

"Cloning's Historical Timeline." National Science Teachers Association, accessed February 7, 2018. http://www.nsta.org/images/news/legacy/scope/0603/cloningtimeline.pdf.

Coghlan, Andy. "Two 'Ethical' Ways to Harvest Stem Cells." *New Scientist*, October 16, 2005. https://www.newscientist.com/article/dn8164-two-ethical-ways-to-harvest-stem-cells.

Cohmer, Sean. "Nuclear Transplantation." The Embryo Project Encyclopedia, June 14, 2011. https://embryo.asu.edu/pages/nuclear-transplantation.

"The Discovery of DNA." Your Genome, accessed February 7, 2018. https://www.yourgenome.org/stories/the-discovery-of-dna.

Eilperin, Juliet. "Female Sharks Can Reproduce Alone, Researchers Find." *Washington Post*, May 23, 2007. http://www.washingtonpost.com/wpdyn/content/article/2007/05/22/AR2007052201405.html.

Enescu, Aurelia, et al. "Ethical Considerations on Human Cloning." *Current Health Sciences Journal*, Fall 2017. http://www.chsjournal.org/archive/vol37-no3-2011/for-practitioner/ethical-considerations-on-human-cloning.

Fisher, Lawrence M. "Cloned Animals Offer Companies a Faster Path to New Drugs." *New York Times*, February 24, 1997. http://www.nytimes.com/1997/02/24/us/cloned-animals-offer-companies-a-faster-path-to-new-drugs.html.

"The Francis Crick Papers." National Institutes of Health, accessed February 7, 2018. https://profiles.nlm.nih.gov/SC/Views/Exhibit/narrative/doublehelix.html.

Highfield, Roger. "Dolly Creator Prof Ian Wilmut Shuns Cloning." *Telegraph*, November 16, 2007. http://www.telegraph.co.uk/news/science/science-news/3314696/Dolly-creator-Prof-Ian-Wilmut-shuns-cloning.html.

"The History of Cloning." Genetic Science Learning Center, accessed February 7, 2018. http://learn.genetics.utah.edu/content/cloning/clonezone.

"Human Cloning." The Center for Bioethics and Culture Network, accessed February 7, 2018. http://www.cbc-network.org/issues/faking-life/human-cloning.

Kolata, Gina. "Scientist Reports First Cloning Ever of Adult Mammal." *New York Times*, February 23, 1997. http://www.nytimes.com/1997/02/23/us/scientist-reports-first-cloning-ever-of-adult-mammal.html.

Lee, Kevin. "What Happens When Something in a Food Chain Goes Extinct." *Seattle Post-Intelligencer*, accessed February 7, 2018. http://education.seattlepi.com/happens-something-food-chain-goes-extinct-4656.html.

Lehrman, Sally. "Is It Time to Give Up on Therapeutic Cloning? A Q & A with Ian Wilmut." *Scientific American*, July 22, 2008. https://www.scientificamerican.com/article/theraputic-cloning-discussion-ian-wilmut.

Lovgren, Stefan. "Stem Cells Can Be Collected Without Destroying Embryos, Scientists Show." *National Geographic News*, August 28, 2006. https://news.nationalgeographic.com/news2006/08/060823-stem-cells.html.

"Mad Cow Disease Fast Facts." CNN Health, June 4, 2017. http://www.cnn.com/2013/07/02/health/mad-cow-disease-fast-facts/index.html.

Marks, Gene. "For Only $50,000 This Texas Company Will Clone Your Pet." *Washington Post*, November 16, 2017. https://www.washingtonpost.com/news/on-small-business/wp/2017/11/16/for-only-50000-this-texas-company-will-clone-your-pet/?utm_term=.8f5ac655a8e3.

Murnaghan, Ian. "New Harvesting Techniques." Explore Stem Cells, May 10, 2017. http://www.explorestemcells.co.uk/newharvestingtechniques.html.

Orf, Darren. "10 Awesome Accidental Discoveries." *Popular Mechanics*, June 26, 2013. http://www.popularmechanics.com/science/health/g1216/10-awesome-accidental-discoveries/.

Perry, Philip. "Startup Promises Immortality Through AI, Nanotechnology, and Cloning." Big Think, May 7, 2017. http://bigthink.com/philip-perry/startup-promises-immortality-through-ai-nanotechnology-and-cloning.

Rothman, Lily. "This Is How Dolly the Sheep Was Cloned." *Time*, July 5, 2016. http://time.com/4384947/dolly-sheep-cloning-history.

Sample, Ian. "Dolly's Clones Aging No Differently to Naturally Conceived Sheep, Study Finds." *Guardian*, July 26, 2016. https://www.theguardian.com/science/2016/jul/26/dollys-clones-ageing-no-differently-to-naturally-conceived-sheep-study-finds.

Seidel, George. "20 Years After Dolly: Cloning Past, Present and Future." KQED Science, February 28, 2017. https://ww2.kqed.org/futureofyou/2017/02/28/20-years-after-dolly-what-cloning-taught-us-and-where-research-is-heading-next.

"Stem Cells: What They Are and What They Do." Mayo Clinic, accessed February 7, 2018. https://www.mayoclinic.org/tests-procedures/bone-marrow-transplant/in-depth/stem-cells/art-20048117.

Tirabassi, Rebecca. "Foundations of Molecular Cloning—Past, Present and Future." New England BioLabs, accessed February 7, 2018. https://www.neb.com/tools-and-resources/feature-articles/foundations-of-molecular-cloning-past-present-and-future.

Wang, Serenitie, Matt Rivers, and Shunhe Wang. "Chinese Firm Clones Gene-Edited Dog in Bid to Treat Cardiovascular Disease." CNN Health, December 27, 2017. https://www.cnn.com/2017/12/25/health/china-dog-cloning-for-disease-intl/index.html.

"What Is Cloning?" Genetic Science Learning Center, accessed February 7, 2018. http://learn.genetics.utah.edu/content/cloning/whatiscloning.

"What Is DNA?" National Institutes of Health, accessed February 7, 2018. https://ghr.nlm.nih.gov/primer/basics/dna.

Index

Page numbers in **boldface** are illustrations.